VICTIMS
NO
MORE

VICTIMS
NO
MORE

by

Thomas R. McCabe, Ph.D.

First published, May, 1978

ISBN: 0-89486-049-6
Library of Congress Catalog Card Number: 77-94792
Printed in the United States of America

Editor's Note:
   Hazelden Educational Materials offers a variety of information on chemical dependency and related areas. Our publications do not necessarily represent Hazelden or its programs,
nor do they officially speak for any Twelve Step organization.

For Dad and Mom

Contents

Author's Note

Before reading these pages, one should be familiar with certain terms:

1. *"He"* vs. *"she"* — For the sake of convenience, this book uses the pronoun "he" to refer to the problem drinker. There are, however, nearly as many women as there are men who are problem drinkers.

2. *"Alcohol"* vs. *"other chemicals"* — One chemical, alcohol, is the focus of this discussion. There are other mood-changing drugs, especially the sedatives, which can produce the same kind of dependency.

3. *"Problem drinker"* vs. *"alcoholic"* — Here the term "problem drinker" can refer to a person before he develops alcoholism, or it may be synonymous with "alcoholic."

4. *"Biological"* vs. *"extended"* family — This book focuses on the "biological" family, namely, the father, mother, sons, and daughters. Anyone at all who knows and cares about a problem drinker is a member of his "extended" family, however, and therefore suffers detrimental effects.

Introduction

The latter half of the twentieth century has brought with it many sources of stress which cause tremendous tension and anxiety within the family, the basic social unit of society. Trying desperately to adapt to the rapid changes of current technology, the family makes continual adjustments to the pressures of modern living. Social critics speculate that the family as a unit may fail to survive the buffetings, drastic shifts in behavior, and expectations which the future will bring.

Add to these external sources of stress the *internal* tension which problem drinking generates within a particular family unit, and there is grave doubt about the ability of that family to continue to function and survive. Problem drinking creates havoc with roles, responsibilities, relationships, and communications within the family system. Under such continued stress, the family system will quickly lose the equilibrium necessary to sustain itself and will soon become nonfunctional.

There are a number of readable books about problem

drinking. They include *Marty Mann Answers Your Questions about Drinking and Alcoholism*, *Marty Mann's New Primer on Alcoholism*, and *America's Worst Drug Problem: Alcohol*, by Richard Reilly. These books focus on the drinker and what happens to him physically and psychologically as his drinking becomes progressively worse.

Every problem drinker, however, affects adversely the lives of at least three other human beings around him. This book is written for those unfortunate people — especially the spouse and children. All family members interact in the degenerative process and become components in a "family system disease."

The nondrinking members of the system lose touch with themselves in the same way the drinker does, and by an insidious process they become victims, enmeshed solidly in the drinking problem.

Ironically, family members are unaware that they may be perpetuating the situation that is destroying them.

Family members need not remain passive, helpless victims. They can learn to understand how the drinking problem involves them intimately, how they aid in maintaining it, and how they can be the instruments for constructive change — and be victims no more.

CHAPTER I

The Family System

(Change As a Function of the System)

During the past several years, the American public has learned a great deal about the facts of problem drinking. A new kind of awareness has shattered many of the myths and dispelled the misconceptions connected with this growing national tragedy. Most people realize, for example, that the overwhelming majority of problem drinkers are not skid row derelicts, but have jobs and families and come from all educational and economic levels.

There still remains, however, a peculiar tendency to view the problem as if it develops in a vacuum. Society assumes blithely that alcohol abuse involves and destroys only the drinker himself, and that the family suffers no devastating effects. Most people believe that wives and children must remain passive, watching helplessly as the drinker sinks into the deadly whirlpool of alcohol abuse. In fact, nothing is further from the truth. Problem drinking does not — and cannot — develop and maintain itself in a vacuum, and family members can take constructive action to halt the steady, progressive destruction of the drinker and themselves.

Before family members can appreciate the extent of their involvement, however, as well as their power to precipitate positive change, it is imperative that they understand fully the concept and dynamics of a "system." By viewing the family as a system, members can see clearly how completely the drinking affects them, and they, in turn, influence the drinking. The following explanation of the concept of a system explains why this approach to problem drinking is so important.

Systems

The dictionary gives multiple definitions and shades of meaning to the word "system." A system can be, for example, an "assemblage of objects united by some form of regular interaction or interdependence." Another definition refers to a system as "an organic or organized whole." Examples might be a telephone system or the solar system.

In the biological sense, a system is "those organs collectively which contribute toward one of the more important and complex vital functions. "The digestive system, circulatory system, nervous system, and even the human body as a whole offer examples of this use of the word."[1]

All these definitions of the word "system" have three common denominators. All systems:

1. consist of units, components, members, or parts.
2. have units, components, members, or parts which are interdependent. That is, they rely upon one another to function properly as a unit.
3. have units, components, members, or parts which are organized to accomplish a specific function or purpose. The units, therefore, must maintain a level of equilibrium or balance. They must work together toward their goal.

Laws of a System

All systems are subject to certain basic laws:

1. The system-as-a-whole is an entity and is greater than the sum of its parts.

2. Anything which affects the system as a whole affects each individual unit within the system.
3. Any change in one unit affects all other units individually and the system as a whole.[2]

Stress within a System

These laws show clearly that whenever one part of any system changes, the alteration introduces strain or stress into the whole and forces the rest of the system to adapt itself or modify its behavior in some way. There are many examples of this principle in daily life. When stress exists in some part of an inorganic system, such as a complex machine, there are warning signals. A factory worker who hears an unusual noise coming from the machine he operates concludes quickly that something is wrong. If someone does not repair it, his whole machine may become dysfunctional. In an organic system such as the human body, the distressing experience of pain may be an important symptom of internal stress. Something is wrong within the system of the body. In an office, when one clerical worker is absent, other employees must bear the added burden of doing his work as well as their own, so that the business can continue to function smoothly and the job gets done.

The Family System

These examples make it easier to view the family as simply another system. The laws of systems in general apply clearly to the family and its functioning:
1. The family consists of a number of members — father, mother, sons, and daughters.
2. There are relationships among these members and they are dependent upon one another.
3. The members function in their roles to accomplish certain purposes, such as fulfilling material needs for food, shelter, clothing, socializing and educating children, and developing an identity and self-esteem.

Laws of the Family System
The family is subject also to certain basic principles which determine its equilibrium:

1. All members assume specific roles and relate to each other in characteristic ways.
2. The roles which family members adopt and the ways they relate to each other operate according to a set of rules. These roles and patterns of relationships constitute the family equilibrium.
3. Any shifts in the family equilibrium (such as the devastating changes which take place when a member begins drinking excessively) may evoke resistance from the family system which is seeking to maintain its stability.
4. No matter how sick or abnormal it may appear to the outsider, the established pattern of equilibrium represents the valiant attempt of the family to minimize threats of pain and disruption.[3]

Stress within the Family System
As with any other system, changes in the operation (the behavior) of one member creates stress for the family as a whole. Since the components of a family system are people, and people are changing constantly (growing and making new decisions), a certain amount of stress will always exist. Most families develop their own problem-solving techniques to cope and function with this stress.

If a husband becomes unemployed, for example, or if unexpected bills pile up, the wife may find a part-time job. The oldest daughter begins doing additional household chores, and junior must take the bus home from school because Mon cannot pick him up. Thus, a change for one person creates changes for everyone else.

Don and Sharon Wegscheider, family therapists at the Johnson Institute, offer an excellent analogy to illustrate the concept of a family as a system:

A family resembles a mobile. A mobile is an art form made up of rods and strings upon which are hung various substances. The beauty of the mobile is in its balance and its movement. The mobile has a way of responding to changing circumstances, such as wind. It changes positions, but always maintains balance. If I flick one of the suspended elements and give it kinetic energy, the whole system moves and gradually brings itself to equilibrium. The same thing is true of a family. In a family where there is stress, a new arrival, or some change, the whole organism shifts to bring peace, stability, or survival. This is the type of reality each of us entered when we came into a family.[4]

The Family System and Problem Drinking

It is essential for anyone who wants to deal effectively with a problem drinker to have a basic understanding of the concept of a system, the laws of systems in general, and the workings of the family system in particular. Only by placing the problem drinker into the perspective of a family systems model can one begin to realize that he does not exist in isolation; he is an integral part of a troubled group of people who are all in equally desperate need of help. Treatment for problem drinking seldom has lasting benefits unless the drinker *and* the rest of the family system receive help.

When one member of the family system begins to abuse alcohol, the result is a progressive series of gradual, insidious changes which cause severe stress for the entire family system. The destructive behavior of the drinker, which is a symptom of his illness, creates a crippling dysfunction for every member of the family. Each time the drinker changes, the rest of the family must adapt to the painful stress which his new behavior produces. Sometimes the strategies they develop are sadly ineffective, and even if these methods do produce temporary results, they ultimately create more problems than they solve.

Because the disruption of family equilibrium produces intolerable stress, the wife of the drinker learns to evade further change temporarily by denying or covering up the behavior of her husband. Unknowingly, however, she perpetuates his drinking by avoiding the problem. The teen-aged son may adapt by drinking abusively himself, by devising excuses to stay away from the house, or by withdrawing from everyday communication with his father even during the times when Dad is sober.

The typical behaviors of the problem drinker and some of the common reactions (adjustments) of other members of the family system cause difficulties for the entire family. Problem drinking creates:

Embarrassment in Social Situations — Members of the family learn quickly to avoid the painful humiliation which drunkenness creates by refusing social invitations. The wife may lie, cover up, and make excuses so she will not have to attend further gatherings. As she withdraws from her friends, she becomes tragically isolated and lonely.

Personality Changes — The drinker may be Dr. Jekyll one minute and Mr. Hyde the next. Completely bewildered by his erratic behavior, the wife may abandon her vain efforts to predict how her husband will react to things. There is a gradual, heartbreaking loss of communication between them.

Family Quarrels — Violent arguments erupt over trivial and insignificant matters. Rather than risk even the remote chance of a quarrel, family members become extremely cautious about what they say, causing most of the conversation in the household to cease.

Frequent Absences from Work — This more advanced symptom of a drinking problem places the wife in a disturbing quandary. She struggles painfully with herself, trying to decide whether or not she should telephone the boss and lie for her husband.

Inconsistent Discipline with the Children — The drinker may severely reprimand his children for misbehavior one time and be totally unconcerned about the same offense another time. Utterly confused by this distressing inconsistency, children become uncertain about what behavior is acceptable.

Memory Losses — As the drinker begins to forget things more and more often, family members wonder whether they should risk reminding him of a Saturday baseball game or a Sunday picnic. While they do not want him to spoil their plans, the suggestion that he has forgotten may cause him to become unreasonably outraged.

Verbal Threats and Physical Abuse — Family members become deeply afraid of him and uncertain of how to react. The wife wonders desperately whether to call the police, leave him, or just forget about his behavior.

Loss of Income — The drinker squanders more and more money on alcohol. The wife may try to deal with the added financial burden by going to work outside the home.

Legal Involvements — Assault and battery charges or drunk driving arrests may be the distressing results of continued drinking. Fearful of her husband's wrath, the wife bails him out of jail. This allows him to avoid accepting the consequences of his actions.

The symptomatic behaviors of the problem drinker grow progressively worse and happen more frequently. This results in added fear, anxiety, distrust, anger, pressure, guilt, and uncertainty for each member of the family. When drinking reaches this stage, it is no longer the problem of a particular person. The entire family system begins quickly to deteriorate. As the problem drinker becomes emotionally and physically sicker, other family members become ill also, because they are integral parts of his system.

If the drinking continues, relationships change gradually among family members. The difficult situation may force them to switch roles and reassign various responsibilities. The drinker ceases to serve as a healthy role-model for the children, and the family becomes totally out of balance and diseased. No one can cope. Family members fail to think clearly, and they react to stress by learning and repeating maladaptive, repetitive, self-defeating behavior.

Facts about Problem Drinking

Some hard, cold statistics give testimony to the disturbing extent of problem drinking:

- There are an estimated 9 million problem drinkers in our country.
- Fifty percent of all highway fatalities involve a drinking driver.
- Forty percent of all male admissions to state hospitals are problem drinkers.
- Thirty-three percent of all suicides are problem drinkers. (Their suicide rate is fifty-eight times greater than the general population.)
- Problem drinkers cause a loss in productivity that costs industry an appalling 10 billion dollars a year.
- Problem drinking accounts for more than one-third of all arrests.

All of the above statistics have received considerable attention in the last ten years, so the general public is becoming more aware of the problem drinker. The destructive effects of alcohol abuse on the spouse and children, however, have gone virtually unnoticed and have been statistically ignored.

Effects of Problem Drinking on the Family

Some facts that are not so well known include the following statistics:

- More than half of juvenile delinquents come from families where there is a problem drinker.
- In more than half the divorce cases in the country, excessive drinking is a major causative factor.
- A governmental agency (NIAAA) reports that over 28 million children suffer ill effects caused by parental problem drinking.
- Between 15 and 20 percent of all applications to some family agencies involve drinking problems.

- At least 80 percent of the children of alcoholic parents suffer disabling emotional problems.

- The University of Washington found recently that there is a high incidence of birth defects in babies of alcoholic women.

Only in the past year or so has the realization of the astronomical cost of alcohol abuse in dollars and human suffering spurred efforts on behalf of those affected by problem drinking.

A recently-formed organization in New York City called "The Other Victims of Alcoholism" offers new hope to those who live with a problem drinker. The founder of this group, Josie Couture, states:

> We must begin to address the needs of the estimated forty million children, men, and women in the United States whose lives are directly and adversely affected by someone else's drinking problem.
> We must also begin to look at the "domino effect" of the impact of alcoholism on family courts; child abuse; battered wives; juvenile delinquency cases; divorce cases; welfare cases; schools; industry; unions; insurance; criminal courts; prisoners; mental institutions; hospitals; governmental agencies; and all other helping services.[5]

The diagram on page 10 illustrates clearly the devastating effect of this "domino effect." Problem drinking creates difficulties for many people besides the drinker himself.

Questions about Problem Drinking

Alcohol abuse causes misery and despair for thousands of families. Here are twenty questions that can help to determine whether or not a drinking problem exists within a given family:

1. Do you lose sleep because of a problem drinker?

2. Do most of your thoughts revolve around the problem drinker or problems that arise because of him or her?

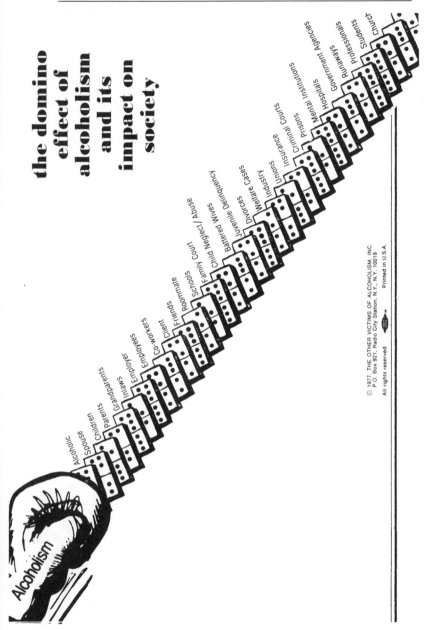

the domino effect of alcoholism and its impact on society

Alcoholic · Spouse · Children · Parents · Grandparents · Inlaws · Employer · Employees · Co-workers · Client · Friends · Roommate · Schools · Family Court · Child Neglect/Abuse · Battered Wives · Juvenile Delinquency · Divorces · Welfare Cases · Industry · Unions · Insurance · Criminal Courts · Prisons · Mental Institutions · Hospitals · Government Agencies · Runaways · Professionals · Students · Church

Alcoholism

NOTE: Reprinted by permission of The Other Victims of Alcoholism (New York: The Other Victims of Alcoholism, 1977). © 1977 by The Other Victims of Alcoholism.

3. Do you extract promises about the drinking which are not kept?

4. Do you make threats or decisions and not follow through on them?

5. Has your attitude changed toward this problem drinker (alternating between love and hate)?

6. Do you mark, hide, dilute, and/or empty bottles of liquor or medication?

7. Do you think that everything would be o.k. if only the problem drinker would stop or control the drinking?

8. Do you feel alone — fearful — anxious — angry and frustrated most of the time? Are you beginning to feel dislike for yourself and to wonder about your sanity?

9. Do you find your moods fluctuating wildly as a direct result of the problem drinker's moods and actions?

10. Do you feel responsible and guilty about the drinking problem?

11. Do you try to conceal, deny, or protect the problem drinker?

12. Have you withdrawn from outside activities and friends because of embarrassment and shame over the drinking problem?

13. Have you taken over many chores and duties that you would normally expect the problem drinker to assume — or that were formerly his or hers?

14. Do you feel forced to try to exert tight control over the family expenditures with less and less success — and are financial problems increasing?

15. Do you feel the need to justify your actions and attitudes and, at the same time, feel somewhat smug and self-righteous compared to the drinker?

16. If there are children in the house, do they often take sides with either the problem drinker or the spouse?

17. Are the children showing signs of emotional stress, such as — withdrawing — having trouble with authority figures — rebelling — acting-out sexually?

18. Have you noticed physical symptoms in yourself, such as — nausea — a "knot" in the stomach — ulcers — shakiness — sweating palms — bitten fingernails?

19. Do you feel utterly defeated — that nothing you can say or do will move the problem drinker? Do you believe that he or she can't get better?

20. Where this applies, is your sexual relationship with a problem drinker affected by feelings of revulsion? Do you "use" sex to manipulate — or refuse sex to punish him or her?[6]

If family members answer "yes" to fewer than three of these questions they probably do not suffer from the destructive effects of a drinking problem. Three or more "yes" answers indicate strongly that someone in the family is indeed a problem drinker and that his behavior is producing dangerous, negative changes in the entire group.

Families may be painfully aware that there is a problem without knowing how to deal constructively with it. They continue in the disheartening and erroneous belief that they are powerless until the drinker asks for help.

The following chapters discuss family reactions to an alcohol problem and tell how, unknowingly, loved ones may actually help to maintain the drinking behavior. Taking constructive action can break the deadly cycle and lead to a renewal of health and stable family relationships.

NOTES

Chapter I

1. *Webster's New Collegiate Dictionary*, s.v. "System."
2. Melville Gooderham, "The Therapy of Relationships," *Addictions*, p. 59.
3. *Alcoholism and the Family*, Fairfield Plan, no. 5, p. 1.
4. Don and Sharon Wegscheider, *Family Illness: Chemical Dependency*, p. 1.
5. Josie Couture, "News Bulletin," p. 2.
6. Betty Reddy, *Alcoholism: A Family Illness*, pp. 9–10.

How the Family System Reacts

(The Drinker Changes, the Family Reacts)

Problem drinking causes changes in behavior in every member of the family. Understanding how a family system functions makes it easier to take a detailed look at these changes. The family as a whole tries vainly to adjust to the problem, and the drinker himself experiences several painful stages in his downward spiral into the depths of the bottle.

The devastating changes resulting from problem drinking affect the entire family. Because the spouse and children play different roles, however, they suffer separate kinds of agony. Each member of the group is in desperate need of help, and, as in any system, a change in any one of them necessitates change in all the rest.

The Family As a Whole

Joan K. Jackson studied several thousand families of problem drinkers and found a fairly predictable set of seven stages that a family goes through in its attempt to adjust to problem drinking:

Stage I — *The Family Attempts to Deny the Problem*

The wife may talk to her husband about his behavior and her growing embarrassment in social situations, but she continues to accept his explanations. Other members of the system get caught up with his rationalizations. The wife may even think that she might somehow be causing his excessive drinking or be exaggerating and overreacting to his drinking. The family denies the problem in the same way the drinker denies it. Their denial represents a hopeless attempt to preserve the family equilibrium. It also helps the family members protect their own self-esteem. By refusing to admit that the drinker has a problem, family members do not have to examine the possibility that they may be contributing to it or that there may be something wrong with them.

Stage II — *The Family Tries to Eliminate the Problem*

As the problem drinking becomes worse, it produces further changes in behavior. Family members begin to withdraw from social situations and isolate themselves. They turn down dinner invitations and become increasingly ashamed and fearful of seeking outside help. They protect the problem drinker by covering up for him to the neighbors or his employer. They tell friends that "he's rundown and not feeling well right now." At the same time, family members take matters into their own hands and attempt to control the situation with home remedies such as threats, extracting promises, hiding or pouring out liquor, or making deals.

The drinking quickly becomes the central focus of all the interrelationships within the family, and anxiety and tension grow acute. The responses of family members to each other become strained and inconsistent. The wife suffers a growing loss of self-esteem, which affects her interaction with the children.

Stage III — *The Family Becomes Disorganized*

The family experiences immobilizing fear, and members despair of finding a solution to their problems. The nagging arguments and threats continue, but no one knows how to meet the problems constructively. Communication is minimal. The children are often caught between the parents and suffer the bewildering dilemma of having to take sides against one or the other of the people who are most important to them. The spouse responds to the lack of affection by avoiding sexual contact and then is accused of being frigid or unfaithful. Family members often become the victims of physical violence as well as the deep psychological pain caused by continued verbal abuse.

Stage IV — *The Family Attempts to Reorganize*

At this stage, there is extreme dysfunction within the family. The wife picks up the reins in a desperate attempt to restore some semblance of equilibrium to the system. She reluctantly shoulders the added burden of her husband's responsibilities, assuming the roles of budget manager, disciplinarian, and family decision-maker. The problem drinker, meanwhile, remains bewilderingly inconsistent in his behavior, trying one minute to buy affection and the next minute delivering stern lectures and threatening his family.

Stage V — *The Family Attempts to Escape the Problem*

Despairing of a return to normal family relationships, the wife begins to consider separation or divorce. She suffers agonizing emotional problems in the process of reaching her decision. A myriad of fears and difficulties plague her. She worries about the future, loss of income, relocation, retaliation by her husband, and the attitudes of the children.

Stage VI — *The Family Escapes the Problem*

If the drinking continues, divorce or separation may become a painful reality. The spouse endures considerable guilt, believing she has deserted a "sick" man. Without his burdensome presence, however, the family begins to reorganize and usually becomes a functional unit once more.

Stage VII — *The Family Reorganizes after the Problem Drinker Seeks Treatment*

If the problem drinker seeks treatment, it is possible for the complete family system to begin to recover also. Unless the entire family undergoes treatment along with the drinker, however, there is little chance that Stage VII will succeed. *It is not simply a matter of treating the problem drinker. It is the family system as a whole which is now "sick" and needs help.*[1]

Terence Williams, Coordinator of the Family Program at the Hazelden Foundation, offers another way of looking at the stages that the family goes through in adjusting to problem drinking. He compares these stages with the ones found by Elizabeth Kübler-Ross in her work with terminally ill patients.

Upon first learning of their fatal diseases, terminally ill people refuse to accept the grim diagnosis of the doctor. They deny that they are going to die. The next stage for dying persons is usually to express feelings of anger and self-pity. ("Why me? Why is God doing this?") Dying persons may next try to bargain, or make a deal with the doctor or God. ("Give me until next Christmas.") When bargaining proves futile, they may enter a stage of isolation or depression. They refuse to eat or receive visitors. Finally, some sort of peace comes upon them. They reach the final stage, acceptance of their impending deaths.

The family of the problem drinker goes through similar stages as members learn to accept the end of their relationships with the problem drinker. It is remarkable how closely their feelings parallel the feelings of the terminally ill patient. The family goes through the same process with the drinker as the terminal patient does with the knowledge of his impending death.

Family members will first deny, or greatly minimize, the fact that there is a problem. They may see it, but they are so fearful that they deny that it is happening. When denial fails dismally, they begin trying homemade remedies to fix or contain the problem. They become violently angry at the drinker and themselves. "We don't have to put up with this," they insist indignantly. Although they threaten the drinker, they seldom take positive action.

Next, they bargain or make deals with him. "Just drink at home." "Straighten up so we don't have to commit you," they plead. When that does not work, they isolate themselves. Their withdrawal leads to further anger and depression.

Finally, if family members get help from Al-Anon or alcoholism counseling services, they can reach the acceptance stage. They realize at last that they are powerless to control the problem drinker's consumption of alcohol, and they accept the fact that they cannot change him. They learn that their only hope is to change themselves, which, in turn, may force the drinker to take positive action also.[2]

The Problem Drinker

A number of publications have discussed in detail the symptoms through which a problem drinker progresses. These publications include *Marty Mann's New Primer on Alcoholism* and *America's Worst Drug Problem: Alcohol*, by Richard Reilly. In these books, the symptoms of alcoholism are categorized into three stages: the prodromal or early stage, the acute or middle stage, and the chronic, terminal stage. It is helpful for the family to understand these stages, but because the problem drinker is not the primary focus here, this discussion will review the symptoms in a simple manner. One can think of the problem drinker as progressing through four stages, with the last two requiring the most attention.

Stage 1. *Avoiding Reference to Drinking*

In the early years, the problem drinker will generally avoid all references to how much he drinks. If someone mentions the subject, he will artfully brush it off and try to change the topic of discussion. In answer to the remark, "You were really putting that booze away again last night at the football game," the drinker will respond, "Oh, that was really an exciting game, wasn't it? Do you think our team has a chance to win the conference?" He will cleverly dodge any questions about his drinking.

Stage 2. *Rebelliousness*

In later years, perhaps because the drinker feels guilty and has grown more defensive about his drinking, the same remarks usually evoke an angry retort: "Mind your own business! You don't do badly yourself!" Or, "Get off my back. I've got a lot of family (or business) problems right now that you wouldn't understand." He will try his best to create alibis and blame others for his drinking.

Stage 3. *Compliance*

Eventually, because of pressure from outside sources, he may enter one of the next two stages, compliance or surrender. The difference between compliance and surrender is extremely important, yet it is sometimes difficult to tell one from the other. Unless the drinker achieves true surrender, however, there will be no chance of recovery from problem drinking.

Surrender and compliance are exceedingly difficult to distinguish because outwardly, they look deceptively alike. Dr. Harry Tiebout has written a great deal about distinguishing these two states. Dr. Tiebout sees compliance as submission, a stage where the drinker accepts his problem consciously, but rejects it in his unconscious mind.[3] The person knows his drinking has defeated him for the moment, but he still nourishes a hope that someday he will be able to consume alcohol normally. Inside, he is still fighting. There is no real acceptance of his condition. He may get into treatment at this point by agreeing to submit to the wishes or demands of his family or his employer, but unless he can get himself to the "surrender" stage, he will achieve few permanent gains from treatment. Compliance, in other words, is only partial surrender.

Stage 4. *Surrender*

Surrender involves nothing less than a *wholehearted accept-ance* of his condition. Surrender is a positive, vital step beyond mere recognition, admission, and compliance. The act of sur-render helps the drinker escape his inner torment and frees him to respond genuinely to available help. The difference between the two words "compliance" and "surrender" is the difference between giving something lip service and really believing it. Within the problem drinker, there are ego factors such as pride, a feeling of omnipotence, and stubbornness. These ego factors resist surrender to his condition. The prob-lem drinker must wrestle with his ego factors and come to terms with himself before he surrenders.

Compliance and surrender look alike outwardly. They are much like the old cowboy gunfights on T.V. After shooting at one another, one side may wave the white flag, indicating that they are giving up. Outwardly, it appears they are surrender-ing. The other side approaches triumphantly, only to find out that the person waving the white flag has a gun hidden behind his back. It is a trick. He has not really given up. Compliance, like the white flag, has only the appearance of surrender.

The difference between these two stages involves many im-portant implications for the problem drinker and for other family members. The family must resist the temptation of thinking that just because the drinker goes for treatment, everything will automatically be blissful thereafter. If the drinker is getting help for the right reasons and the family is also getting help for the right reasons, then and only then is there a good chance for the family system to begin to get well.

The Wife — Victim or Villain?

Although each marriage is different from every other, spouses of problem drinkers often go through a common set of reactions. The following paragraphs look carefully at these responses.

Just as there have been numerous attempts to study the personalities of problem drinkers, so are there different theories about the personalities of their wives. Some experts suggest that the wife is an aggressive woman who married her husband to fulfill her own need to be dominant, while others believe she is emotionally normal and healthy until her husband begins to be a problem drinker and forces her to make destructive changes in her personality. Still other experts agree that the truth lies somewhere between these theories.[4]

These conjectures, however, have little to do with helping the family to take constructive action to get the drinker into treatment. Whether or not the personality of a wife contributes to the drinking her husband does is far less important than the way she copes with his disruptive behavior and the roles she plays. Some of the research done in this area will give an idea of what happens in the family system and will explain some of the ways that spouses deal with problem drinking.

Jane James and Morton Goldman, from the University of Missouri, studied the behaviors that wives use to cope with husbands who drink too much. The women watched helplessly while their spouses plunged from social drinking into excessive or alcoholic drinking. These wives exhibited behaviors which fell into one of five categories:

1. *Withdrawal within Marriage* — The wife may quarrel with her husband about his drinking or choose to avoid him. She may experience disturbing feelings of anger and helplessness.

2. *Protection* — She pours out liquor or hides bottles in a vain effort to curb his problem drinking. She mothers him, seeing that he eats or fixing him a drink to ease his hangover. She may ask his employer to intervene in the problem.

3. *Attack* — She vents her anger by locking him out, threatening him with separation, or pretending that she herself is drunk, in a hostile attempt to get even with him.

4. *Safeguarding Family Interests* — Fraught with financial difficulties, she tries doling out money to her husband or hiding it from him. She pays his debts to avoid disgrace and borrows money when none is left. Trying desperately to avoid conflict, she keeps the children out of his way.
5. Acting out — The wife may get drunk herself, try to make her husband jealous, ridicule him, or threaten suicide.[5]

Among other things, the study revealed that women coped most frequently with their husbands' problem drinking by withdrawing within their marriages. The researchers felt that their findings tended to support Joan K. Jackson's theory about the adjustments of the family to the different stages of abusive drinking.

Other researchers have also studied the different roles a wife may play as she responds to the problem drinking of her husband. Dr. Martin Goldberg, a psychiatrist at the University of Pennsylvania, found seven different roles that wives adopt to deal with excessive drinking within the family. He labels them as:

The Scapegoat: She takes the blame for her husband's drinking. She is convinced that he drinks because of his unhappiness with her. She considers herself hopelessly inadequate as a woman and a wife. He, of course, is delighted to have her as a scapegoat.

The Coverup Artist: She tries desperately to hide the problem, believing that she is protecting her husband and her family. She calls up the boss and lies for her spouse, declines social invitations, and hides the drinking from the children by explaining that their father is "exhausted" or "sick."

The Minimizer: She not only covers up, but also joins her husband in the denial of his alcoholism. She explains frequently, "He doesn't drink any more than a lot of people," or "He just likes to have a good time once in awhile."

The Maximizer: She inflates the drinking far beyond its actual dimensions. She complains, "He drinks like a fish," or "He guzzles morning, noon, and night." Whatever his intake, she is likely to magnify it five- or tenfold. This produces a sense of outrage in the husband and strengthens his denial.

The Drinking Buddy: She drinks along with her husband, rationalizing that she wants to protect him. In actual fact, she is an alcoholic herself or on the way to becoming one. The spouses have an unspoken pact that they will not call attention to the excessive drinking done by both of them.

The Saboteur: While she openly urges her husband to stop drinking, she tends to discourage or sabotage any plan for abstinence. She arranges their social activities so they interfere with her husband's attendance at A.A. meetings. She serves large quantities of liquor at social affairs in their home. She is not, however, consciously aware of her subversive acts.

The Provocateur: She bears a similarity to the saboteur, but she goes a step further. She consciously and openly does her best to provoke her husband to excessive drinking, goading him to it by saying, "Go ahead, go out and get drunk again. That's all you're good for," or, "I know what you'll do. You'll drink yourself silly, just as you always do."[6]

None of these roles, of course, is at all helpful in dealing with the problem in the family.

Thelma Whalen, from a family service agency in Dallas, Texas, has written about four common personality types who seek assistance in dealing with a spouse who is a problem drinker:

The Sufferer: "Suffering Susan" has a need to punish herself. The need is so strong that it forms the nucleus of her personality.

The Waverer: "Wavering Winnifred" is likeable, good-natured, and pleasant, but at the same time she is fearful and insecure. She can manage relationships only with people who are inadequate.

The Controller: "Controlling Catherine" dominates all aspects of life with the problem drinker. She is the best decision-maker and often harbors resentful attitudes toward men. She does not want an adequate man, for he would painfully threaten her.

The Punisher: Lastly, there is "Punitive Polly," whose relationship to her husband resembles that of a boa constrictor to a rabbit. Such a relationship is often mutually satisfactory; some rabbits seem to enjoy being swallowed. Quite often, however, the rabbit rebels and goes out and gets drunk.

Polly may be a career woman and/or a clubwoman. Her interest is in the world of business or politics, where she competes aggressively with men. She appears content as long as the problem drinker refrains from embarrassing her socially.[7]

It is not the intention of this chapter to imply a cause-effect relationship between the personality of the wife and the drinking of her spouse. The above references serve only to emphasize and reinforce the fact that when problem drinking exists, the whole family system suffers and becomes intimately involved, not just the drinker, who is usually considered to be the focus of the problem. Unless family members seek help, there is little chance that the cessation of drinking will create any fundamental change in the ineffective functioning of the system.

Whether or not the wife reacts in a manner that fits the above labels or types, it is very probable that she will respond in some ineffective, self-defeating way. The following quotation from Al-Anon literature points out many of these destructive behaviors:

The wife of an alcoholic will probably
- make excuses for her husband's drinking behavior
- keep up appearances — see that he gets a haircut and is properly dressed
- be sure to wake him in time to get to work
- call and tell his employer he's sick — if he can't make it
- cover up for him to the neighbors
- make every effort to get food into him
- stay at home to keep out of sight of other people
- go out as often as possible to get away from it all.

She will often
- do the chores around the place that ought to be done by the man of the house

- work to help the family income along — or else earn all of it
- pay his bills for him*
- buy the things needed for the house*
- control the finances — or as much as she can get her hands on.
- get employment for her husband or help him with his work.

*Mothers do a good bit of these for their alcoholic sons, too!

She may

- drink with him so he won't get so intoxicated
- encourage him to drink at home so he won't get into trouble
- clean up the bed when he vomits — or worse.
- complain about it
- then do it all over again.

Many a wife

- tells him to get out so she won't have to look at him
- then sends the children to bring him home
- goes out to look for him herself, or telephones around to find him
- tells him not to yell at the children or hit them
- then yells at them and hits them herself
- complains that he doesn't love her any more
- denies it when he makes same complaint about her.

The typical wife of an alcoholic will

- resent bitterly, and loudly, the money he spends on liquor
- buy more for him or give him money to buy it
- pour it down the sink
- blame his drinking on his job
- blame it on the Army, the Navy, the Air Force.

She's apt to

- console him when he's feeling sorry for himself
- tell him not to feel so sorry for himself

- use sex as a weapon to control him
- refuse to sleep with him
- sleep with him
- keep on having children by him.

She often

- lies about the amount of money they owe or have on hand
- runs up bills so he won't have enough left to spend on liquor
- tries to tie up his free time so he won't have time to drink
- buys him all kinds of tools and sports equipment to get him interested in something besides drinking
- feels mortally offended when the novelty wears off and he goes back to his bottle.

She'll

- worry over him
- cry over him
- scold him
- mother him
- beat him
- scream at him
- swear at him
- give him the silent treatment
- spend the night in a hotel
- spend it with the neighbors
- threaten to leave him for good
- fail to carry out the threat
- run home to mother
- try to reason with him
- tell him to telephone if he's going to be late
- argue and scold him when he does telephone
- encourage him to try controlled drinking so she won't have to go without hers
- wait on him
- make him wait on himself.

She may

- call the police, go to court and charge him with assault
- and then withdraw the charge
- keep herself and her home spotless
- let herself and the house fall apart
- refuse to take another beating
- take another beating — and another
- beg him not to drive when he drinks
- get him out of the jam he gets into for drunken driving
- cheat on him because he cheated on her.

She'll

- hate him
- hate his mother
- try to get help for him
- cook for him
- refuse to cook for him.

She will

- pray he will quit drinking
- pray he'll drink himself to death
- hope he breaks his neck before she does it for him.

And finally

- some crisis may force her to take the critical step of getting her husband out of the home, or leaving home with the children, to compel him to take action about his drinking.[8]

The Forgotten Children: Innocent Victims

Perhaps the members of the family system who suffer the most serious damage are the sons and daughters.

While gathering material for her book *The Forgotten Children*, Margaret Cork interviewed 115 children with alcoholic parents. The children ranged in age from ten to sixteen years. A significant number of the children felt rejected by both their fathers and mothers. They had great difficulty in making and keeping friends and refused to go to the homes of other children because they felt unable to return the hospitality. Parental fighting and constant quarreling created major problems for the children. One twelve-year-old boy expressed his feelings by saying:

> Mostly I'm by myself — there isn't anyone I really know. We've moved a lot and I don't want to make new friends. Even if I had a friend, I wouldn't bring him home. I wouldn't want him to know what my family is like. I'm afraid he'd hear the fighting or see my dad, and then he wouldn't like me. Mom says we shouldn't tell anyone (about Dad's alcoholism). Anyway, I'd hate for them to know. I'm too ashamed . . . People shouldn't know your business. I wouldn't want them to feel sorry for me.[9]

Herman Krimmel and Helen Spears studied 125 children from families with a drinking problem. The ages of these youngsters ranged from thirteen to twenty-one years. The researchers discovered that:

Most of the children in the study were used as weapons in the war between the alcoholic and nonalcoholic parent.

The children were caught in a bewildering tug of war as each parent tried to get them to side with him or her.

The reorganization of the family frequently forced children to assume adult responsibilities prematurely.

At nine years of age, one boy was told he would have to be the man of the house.

Regardless of the degree of the distortion within the family, violence was almost universal. The younger the child at the onset of violence, the more devastating the effect.

Children witnessed or were victims of uncontrolled parental outbursts.

Children in an alcoholic family developed stunted relationships. This seemed to limit them in achieving a sense of self-worth.

They received little confidence or self-assurance and could not meet the impossible demands placed on them.

Many found it difficult to plan for a career or college because they were conditioned to accept defeat before they started. Others attempted to take refuge in impeccable behavior.[10]

Another recent study reports that there may be over 38,000,000 children in America with an alcoholic parent. Among the cases were:

1. A seven-year-old boy who cooked, cleaned, and kept house for the four younger children in the family.
2. A nine-year-old boy in a protective child care center who ran away periodically to check on his alcoholic mother and make sure she was all right.
3. Parents who revealed to their children the details of their sex lives or the extramarital activities of their spouses.
4. A young boy whose alcoholic father would awaken him in the middle of the night, looking for sympathetic understanding.[11]

In summary, it is painfully obvious that children react to problem drinking in the family system with marked degrees of confusion, guilt, nervousness, anxiety, shame, fear, and resentment. The ravaging effects of problem drinking spare no one in the family system. Attitudes, feelings, and behaviors of all family members change, and roles, relationships, functions, and communications break down disturbingly. The family as a whole becomes diseased.

Louise Mehrman Goodman, Coordinator of Family Services at South Oaks Hospital in Amityville, New York, has developed a good visual summary chart, which appears on pages 30–31, of the devastation which problem drinking creates for the entire family.

Members of the family pour all their energy into dealing with the intolerable drinking situation and the drinker himself. Coping becomes the central part of their lives. Things grow so confusing that instead of taking actions that would be helpful, they respond in ways that, ironically, allow the destructive behavior to continue. The next chapter focuses on how family members perpetuate the drinking by inappropriate responses.

NOTES

Chapter II

1. Joan K. Jackson, "The Adjustments of the Family to the Crisis of Alcoholism," *Quarterly Journal of Studies on Alcohol*, pp. 562–586.
2. Terence Williams, *Free to Care*, pp. 10–12.
3. Harry M. Tiebout, *Surrender Versus Compliance in Therapy with Special Reference to Alcoholism*, p. 3.
4. Patricia Edwards, Cheryl Harvey, and Paul D. Whitehead, "Wives of Alcoholics: A Critical Review and Analysis," *Quarterly Journal of Studies on Alcohol*, pp. 112–132.
5. Jane E. James and Morton Goldman, "Behavior Trends of Wives of Alcoholics," *Quarterly Journal of Studies on Alcohol*, pp. 373–381.
6. Martin Goldberg, "Chronic Alcoholism: Include the Alcoholic and the Spouse in Treatment." *Consultant*, pp. 63–69.
7. Thelma Whalen, "Wives of Alcoholics: Four Types Observed in a Family Service Agency," *Quarterly Journal of Studies on Alcohol*, pp. 632–641.
8. *What Do You Do about the Alcoholic's Drinking?* pp. 1–7.
9. R. Margaret Cork, *The Forgotten Children* (paperback), p. 7.
10. Herman Krimmel and Helen Spears, *The Effect of Parental Alcoholism on Adolescents*, pp. 1–8.
11. Booz, Allen, and Hamilton, Inc., *Final Report on the Needs of and Resources for Children of Alcoholic Parents*, prepared for the National Institute on Alcohol Abuse and Alcoholism, pp. 22–29.

Effects of Alcoholism on the Family

Alcoholic	Family

ATTEMPTS TO DENY THE PROBLEM

Alcoholic:
- drinking episodes fairly infrequent
- shame
- discussion of drinking episode
- promises
- making up, ideal role playing
- recurrent drinking

Family:
- feelings of embarrassment, humiliation
- discussion of drinking episode
- making up, ideal role playing
- false hope
- disappointment, hurt, confusion
- advice seeking from relatives and friends
- trial and error

ATTEMPTS TO ELIMINATE THE PROBLEM

Family:
- social isolation
- loss of perspective
- drinking becomes focus of anxiety
- drinking blamed for all problems
- feelings that they are "different"
- attempts to cover up
- resentments
- lack of communication
- loss of self-worth, feelings of failure
- guilt, false hope, temporary gain in self-worth, euphoria
- efforts to control
- obsession with drinking
- concentration on short-term goals
- attempts to maintain illusion of happy home
- self-pity
- protection of children
- dependence on children for emotional support
- anger and anxiety
- jealousy of children's affection for alcoholic
- attempts to involve children in trying to control the alcoholic
- loss of creativeness

Alcoholic:
- resentments
- lack of communication
- periods of sobriety
- recurrent drinking
- pleasant interactions with children

DISORGANIZATION

Family:
- hopelessness
- skepticism
- tension
- nagging, silent treatment
- children torn in loyalties, confused, terrified
- behavior problems in children
- violence — relief and shame
- compulsive behavior

Alcoholic:
- non-drinking periods
- recurrent drinking
- inconsistent behavior
- unreasonable demands

* EFFORTS TO ESCAPE

Difficulties to overcome:
- where to go, money, avoidance of further violence
- attempts at sobriety and resultant feelings of guilt
- threats of violence or suicide
- children's criticism for staying or

loss of job, violence
avoidance of sex

relatives' antagonism toward alcoholic, and resultant defensiveness
conflicting advice of helping agencies
delays in receiving help

Before decision to separate can be made, wife must:
resolve conflicts about self and husband
give up hope for marriage
find self-confidence to face unknown future
accept failure of marriage
alter all life goals
get rid of feelings of responsibility for the alcoholic
be able to plan for long term future

Outside Help Sought
guilt, loss of self respect and self-confidence
chaos
fear
inability to make decisions and follow through

ATTEMPTS TO REORGANIZE IN SPITE OF PROBLEMS
crisis occurs which requires action (wife returns to work, possible separation, etc.)
wife becomes manager, discipliner, decision-maker, controller, assuming husband and father roles
alcoholic is ignored
reorganization of priorities, with children first
pity for alcoholic
children ignore alcoholic
children's acceptance of drinking as permanent
outside activities increase

attempts to undermine discipline
desperate attempts to regain children's affection
open expression of resentments against children
abuse
feelings of isolation
attempts to enter circle of warmth or smash it

Increase in Money Problems, Violence, Accidents, Illness, Bizarre Behavior
hope is rekindled
hope is destroyed
social agencies frequently consulted
Al Anon — increase in stability and self-worth
no attempts to cover up drinking

attempts to stop drinking
repeated drinking

* EFFORTS TO ESCAPE
decision to separate or divorce due to:
near catastrophes
accumulated problems
emotional problems
practical difficulties
damage to children

RECOVERY
feelings of superiority
resentments
poor communication
fear and lack of trust
reorganization of roles
unrealistic expectations

REORGANIZATION OF WHOLE FAMILY

possible continued violence
continued drunken behavior
same problems as other divorced families with additions:
guilt about deserting sick man
children upset
interference with job and life in general

REORGANIZATION OF PART OF THE FAMILY

NOTE: Reprinted by permission of Louise Mehrman Goodman, © 1975 by Louise Mehrman Goodman. Developed for South Oaks Hospital, Amityville, NY.

How The Family System Maintains The Drinking

(Who Prolongs the Problem?)

> One person cannot become an alcoholic without the help of at least another. It cannot appear in isolation, progress in isolation nor maintain itself in isolation. One person drinks in a way that is completely unlike social drinking. Others react to the drinking and its consequences. The drinker responds to the reaction and drinks again. This sets up a merry-go-round.[1]

The inappropriate responses of the family may actually maintain and perpetuate further drinking episodes. Everyone involved learns sadly ineffective and even destructive behavior patterns with which he or she tries to cope with the stressful situation. This chapter deals with how the problem drinker manages to continue drinking, and how the whole family perpetuates the drinking by getting involved with him in various games.

Defense Mechanisms

Some idea of what defense mechanisms are and the way they work will help promote a clear understanding of how the problem drinker maintains his drinking. Defense mechanisms are learned responses that a person uses to protect himself from strong anxiety and ego threats. All human beings utilize defense mechanisms in their daily lives. Because defense mechanisms reduce anxiety and inner conflicts, they are acceptable, though not necessarily desirable, tools for dealing with stress. When a person employs these mechanisms only occasionally, they tend to protect the integrity of the ego. If one uses them continuously and exclusively, however, they foster self-deception and destroy any chance of working through the underlying problems that cause them to be necessary.

The problem drinker makes frequent use of five common defense mechanisms: *repression, rationalization, displacement, projection*, and especially *denial*.

Repression:

When a person represses his painful feelings, he is no longer consciously aware of them, but they continue to simmer in the subconscious. The problem drinker buries his emotions, setting himself up for serious trouble. Later, usually after consuming alcohol, he will explode violently. Most people repress their emotions at one time or another, but for an alcoholic, doing so can be exceedingly dangerous.

Rationalization

A person justifies his behavior by explaining it away. He may, for example, enter a fast-food restaurant for a hamburger and soft drink, only to discover he has forgotten his wallet. He rationalizes by saying, "Oh well, I wasn't really that hungry anyway." Such a statement reduces disappointment and does no great harm. Confronted by such a rationalization, most people would immediately recognize it for what it was.

The problem drinker, however, abuses this defense mechanism. As his behavior becomes increasingly incongruous with his intentions, he rationalizes outrageously to himself and others. If he planned to have one or two drinks and somehow ends up with six or seven, he will probably justify it by suggesting, "Oh well, it's good to hang one on once in a while. Anybody who works as hard as I do deserves to get drunk." The consequences of rationalizations like these tend to be perilous.

A rationalization, then, is an excuse, or a way of making an unbelievable situation credible. The problem drinker never seems to exhaust his supply of rationalizations. Tragically, while everyone else can see right through these rationalizations, he remains convinced that they are valid. One of the tasks of a treatment program is to present a continual confrontation with the real world and deflate his denial system.

Displacement

An individual vents strong, hostile feelings against a person or object other than the one which aroused the emotions initially. When frustrating events accumulate at work, the problem drinker turns his anger inward or outward. If he turns it inward, he becomes depressed and dangerously upset with himself. He seeks refuge in the bottle, only to discover that alcohol depresses him even further. If he turns his frustration outward, he may release his anger on an object such as his car, resulting in dangerous driving and a possible accident. His wife and children may also become innocent targets of his hostility and suffer verbal or physical abuse from him.

Projection

One places all the blame for one's own unacceptable desires on others. The drinker projects the blame for his alcohol abuse on people, places, or things besides himself, failing to take responsibility for his behavior.

By projection the alcoholic finds in others what is unacceptable in himself. This involves great lack of insight whereby he attempts to rid himself of his intolerable feelings and motives by recognizing them in others. He may interpret their conduct as motivated by feelings that he unconsciously acknowledges as unworthy in himself. He may accuse others of being highly critical, although this describes his own attitude toward himself. The maneuver of projection might cause him to accuse others of wanting him to get drunk, or he may accuse his A A friends of drinking. He also may accuse others of suspecting him of drinking.[2]

R. J. Solberg, the author of this quotation, is talking about projection used during a "dry-drunk" period, which is discussed in a later chapter. This behavior, however, happens throughout the problem drinking days also.

Denial

The individual blocks unpleasant situations by refusing to face their reality. Denial is the key characteristic of the personality of a problem drinker. He tries desperately to refute his outrageous behavior by insisting he has no problem.

It appears to be a law of human behavior that two directly conflicting beliefs cannot co-exist for very long in one individual. As a person's drinking begins to produce adverse results, such a conflict is created. On the one hand, alcohol has become an important and rewarding component of his life. He likes to drink because it produces unusually good feelings and/or helps shut off bad feelings.[3] On the other hand, reality is relentlessly trying to impose awareness of impaired mate and family relations, work efficiency, etc. At this point, there are only two possible resolutions of the conflict: reject drinking or reject reality. Some in fact do select the former, especially if he is one of the lucky few who have important people, such as family members or helping professionals, confronting him with the connection between drinking and undesirable reality. Many more, unfortunately, begin to reject reality, which is obviously the more likely alternative given the remarkable propensity of humans to rationalize whatever behavior they find highly rewarding.[4]

In his book *I'll Quit Tomorrow*, Vern Johnson speaks about another form of denial which he refers to as "euphoric recall." Under the influence of alcohol, the problem drinker will selectively remember his feelings and behavior. He distorts completely the reality of the situation, however, because he recalls only the euphoria he felt, and not the painful or embarrassing part.[5]

Very often the problem drinker expresses denial in very subtle ways. His statements contain or imply "I never." "I never had a drunk-driving charge." "I never drink anything but beer." "I never drink in the morning." "I never miss work." "I never physically abuse my wife or children." These are examples of indirect denial of a drinking problem.

Through continual use of all these defense mechanisms, the problem drinker eventually forms a very highly developed defense system, whereby he becomes almost totally self-deluded and unable to see the truth of his condition. Thus, he maintains his drinking and is tragically unaware of what is happening to him and his family system.

Games Families Play

In order to see how the whole family system gets caught up in the problem of alcohol abuse, one must understand the concept of "games." "Games" are the methods by which the family relates to the problem drinker in a manner which helps to perpetuate his abuse of alcohol.

A game consists of a series of behavior interchanges between at least two people. The purpose of these interchanges is to avoid intimate and legitimate exchanges of feelings. They offer a nonthreatening way for people to pass time together.

There are many games and many different labels for them. In each game, there is a series of behaviors which have a beginning and an end, an ulterior psychological motive, and advantages (payoffs) for everyone involved.

All people consciously or unconsciously play games with others with whom they interact in daily work, social, and home life. They devise strategies to obtain recognition ("strokes") from others. For the most part, games, like defense mechanisms, are acceptable, although not desirable. When the problem drinker plays games, however, they become painfully destructive for both him and his family system.

This chapter exposes some of the more common games involved in problem drinking. Family members will often recognize their roles in a particular game and may decide to do something about the situation.

Eric Berne, in his book *Games People Play*, provides a detailed exposition and analysis of over one hundred games. One of these is called Alcoholic. The drinker plays the central role — the one who is "it." Other roles or players commonly encountered in this game include: the Persecutor, the Rescuer, the Patsy, and the Connection.

The spouse usually plays the chief supporting role as the Persecutor, or the one who berates the problem drinker for his drinking. The spouse can also play the role of Rescuer, begging and pleading with him to stop, or the role of Patsy, helping him undress, getting him an aspirin, or offering him special malt nourishment to build up his health. The family physician or an unsuspecting counselor may also take the role of Rescuer, saving the drinker temporarily for a few weeks or months. The Patsy neither persecutes nor rescues the drinker, but becomes his victim. The local grocer who extends repeated credit may play this role. Bartenders often find themselves in the role of the Connection, for they are the direct source of supply for the drinker. The Connection is in the game for his own profit.[6]

One obvious payoff for the drinker in the game of Alcoholic is that he is able to continue to consume alcohol with impunity. He can also wallow in self-pity, castigating himself and calling himself names during the psychological torment of the hangover.

In his book *Games Alcoholics Play*, Claude Steiner suggests three different variations of the game of Alcoholic. They are

Drunk and Proud (D. & P.), Lush, and Wino. In all three variations, the drinker puts himself into a position of being the object of obvious disapproval so that others who appear initially righteous and innocent end up foolish and full of blame. His position seems to be, "I am not O.K. (and I know it) and you are not O.K. either (but you aren't aware of it). So I'm going to expose you."

Drunk and Proud

D. & P. involves the drinker and another person, whose part alternates between the roles of Persecutor and the Patsy. The drinker tries to make others so angry with him that they show their impotence and foolishness. "The game is often played by salesmen and executives with their wives," says Dr. Steiner, "and for them, the game is to punish the wife for her dominating and possessive attitudes."[7] For example, when a wife reproaches her husband for staying out very late drinking the night before, he appears contrite and apologetic. If she accepts the apology, she puts herself into the Patsy role. If she rejects the apology, she continues as the Persecutor and appears merciless and unkind. Thus, the drinker wins the game by proving that the problem is not his alone. His wife is "not O.K." either. She or anyone else who tries to stop the drinker from misbehaving ends up feeling foolish or very angry.

Lush

In this game, the drinker feels exceedingly sorry for himself because he does not receive "strokes" (praise, appreciative remarks, recognition, or physical expressions of affection). He plays Lush with a partner who is unable, or who finds it difficult, to express positive feelings. The drinker devises other ways of getting his strokes, such as demanding the attention of the Rescuer, who may be a professional therapist or the family physician. A "nobody loves me" position is the central theme of the game. The other members of the family system may play the roles of Persecutor and Rescuer.

Wino

Wino is a very self-destructive game played for exceedingly high stakes. It is often the grim successor of Lush. In Wino, the drinker obtains his strokes by risking health and life itself. He practically forces the legal and social agencies to be his connections to a payoff: a place of shelter and food. By doing this, he demonstrates that his plight must be desperate indeed before anyone will help him or care for him in his sickness.[8]

Richard Bates, Medical Director of the Alcoholism Unit at E. W. Sparrow Hospital, Lansing, Michigan, reviewed and elaborated on some other games mentioned by Berne and Steiner:

Stupid

The drinker refuses to try his best to achieve as much as he can, for fear that his best will not be good enough. He plays stupid and does nothing so no one will expect anything from him.

Wooden Leg

A person who plays this game uses a physical or educational handicap as an excuse for not trying. When some drinkers learn that alcoholism is a disease, they use the fact as an excuse. "What can you expect of me? I have a disease," they mutter self-pityingly. They say, in effect, "I can't help myself."

Kick Me

The drinker bends over, figuratively, and asks someone to kick him. When they oblige and he falls over, he can complain bitterly about what a terrible world this is. He does his best to anger others so they "kick" him, allowing him to cry piteously, "People are always picking on me."

Frigid Woman

This game is an excellent illustration of how the wife of a

drinker can use their sexual relationship in a way that perpetuates the problem drinking. The wife may be angry or resentful about his drinking behavior. She will punish him by first enticing him to the bedroom and then suddenly slamming the door in his face. He gets very angry and frustrated and has a perfect excuse to go out drinking.

Uproar

Uproar often follows closely on the heels of Frigid Woman. The drinker and someone else in the family system argue about finances, in-laws, or discipline of children, resulting in a shouting match which ends when the drinker slams the door and retreats to the bar.[9]

The Merry-Go-Round Named Denial

Joseph L. Kellermann, former Director of the Charlotte, North Carolina, Council on Alcoholism, illustrates another way in which the family may perpetuate problem drinking. He describes the roles that family members play in the destructive, downward spiral of problem drinking in terms of a tragic three-act drama.

In this play, there are at least four characters: the Problem Drinker, the Enabler, the Victim, and the Provocatrix (Adjuster). Family members, neighbors, and friends adopt these roles in real life.

Act I of the play begins with the Problem Drinker in center stage. He becomes gradually dependent on alcohol but continues somehow to convince himself of his independence. He takes great pains to avoid reference to his drinking and to deny it in every way possible. Later in Act I, as he begins to get into trouble socially or legally, he relies upon others to protect him from the unpleasant consequences. Toward the end of the act we see him as a helpless, dependent child.

In Act II, the other characters become seriously involved. As the scene opens, the Problem Drinker is growing completely passive and sinking into a totally dependent state. This sets the stage for the Enabler to make his or her appearance. The Enabler (usually played in real life by ministers, doctors, lawyers, social workers, or counselors) sets out heroically to save the drinker. What actually happens, however, is that the Enabler makes it possible for the drinker to avoid completely the painful consequences of his destructive behavior.

Next, the Victim (usually the boss, superior, or business partner) enters the play. He repeatedly protects and covers up for the drinker. The Victim allows the drinker to hold onto his job safely while he continues his irresponsible behavior.

Finally, the Provocatrix (the wife or mother of the drinker) comes onto the scene. She makes constant, desperate attempts to adjust to the situation and to cope with the drinking. The Provocatrix becomes hurt, upset, guilt-ridden, resentful, and bitter, but she holds the family together valiantly despite all the trouble within the system.

As Act II continues, the people who fall into the above roles do everything for the Problem Drinker, allowing him to accomplish nothing for himself. Alcohol removes his psychic pain, and the family members and friends remove the painful consequences of his drinking.

Act III of the play continues with the Problem Drinker, still experiencing denial, blaming the other members of the family system for his troubles. He manipulates the situation so that he does the drinking and other members of his system bear the burden of guilt. The three other players extract empty promises from him as he continues to drink.

Since the drinker writes the script to the play and receives the rewards, it is to his benefit to prevent it from ending. The drama goes on and on. . . . Act one returns, and the curtain never falls. By getting caught up in game-playing, family members adopt roles that keep the merry-go-round circling endlessly.[10]

Terence Williams describes another way in which the family members become Enablers, or Caretakers for the drinker:

When concerned persons become hooked, they unwittingly accept the role of enabler for the addict. Another way to describe this role is hurt — or angry — or frightened — caretaker for the addict. These family members sometimes become saviors: a healthy, kind, and loving part of them says that they have the responsibility to save the addict ("I know I am a capable person, and I know I can help — if I can just find the answers"); or they become partners, drinking with the addict, trying to join him in his game and to win him over to some reasonable behavior this way. ("Right now he needs me, and we are going to stick together until we have this licked"); or they become victims, the martyrs, and — suffering already from a low self-concept — they assume the self-defeating role of people whose mission in life is to suffer (It's my duty as a wife, husband, parent. . . . I know things will be better someday"); or they become tough guys, trying vainly to force the addict into changing his behavior ("What this kid needs is some military therapy, two years in the service! They'll straighten him out!"). Concerned persons will play one or more of these roles at one time or another; or one of the roles will be their way of relating to the addict. In some way, however, they establish themselves as being responsible for the addict. In each of these roles, there is the implicit assumption that the concerned persons can somehow change the addict, and it is this assumption, together with the addict's defiance, that keeps the game going.[11]

There is, then, an almost endless list of games and roles that the problem drinker and family members use to cope with their difficulties. All the games involve basically the same family interactions. A few of the games and roles were briefly described here to provide some insight into how they operate and how the whole family system, playing various roles, gets caught up in them, resulting in destructive behavior patterns which serve to maintain the deadly cycle of alcohol abuse.

Perhaps the most appropriate word to describe family members is "co-alcoholic." Co-alcoholic is extremely fitting because it connotes the intimate entanglement of the whole extended family in the "dis-ease" of relationships.

They are co-alcoholics when they begin to share the system of delusions, the make-believe world of their alcoholics. They are co-alcoholics when they begin to adjust to the drunken behavior of their alcoholic, to his need for alcohol above everything else. They are co-alcoholics when they begin to feel satisfied if he drinks himself into a stupor and doesn't *bother* anyone else. They are co-alcoholics when they can live day in and day out with this unreliable and unpredictable kind of person just because they can recall that he was not always like that.[12]

Regardless of the term used to describe the roles family members play, unless these people decide to do something positive, the games will go on and on. The actors will continue to perform this tragedy night after night. The merry-go-round will keep circling round and round endlessly.

It will continue until the drinker dies, until he goes insane, or until the family members make a constructive change that forces the drinker to change as well. Once family members see how they are perpetuating the drinker's destructive use of alcohol, they are able to choose to change themselves, which may, in turn, lead to change for the drinker.

How the family members can change themselves, get themselves off the deadly merry-go-round, and perhaps even stop it, is the subject of the next chapter.

NOTES

Chapter III

1. Joseph L. Kellermann, *Alcoholism: A Merry-go-round Named Denial*, p. 5.
2. R. J. Solberg, *The Dry Drunk Syndrome*, pp. 5–6.
3. Richard O. Heilman, *Dynamics of Drug Dependency*, quoted in *Why Do Alcoholics Deny Their Problem?* by Jon R. Weinberg, p. 8. © 1973 by *Minnesota Medicine.* Used by permission of the Minnesota State Medical Association.
4. Weinberg, *Why Do Alcoholics Deny Their Problem?* p. 8. © 1973 by *Minnesota Medicine.* Used by permission of the Minnesota State Medical Association.
5. Vernon E. Johnson, *I'll Quit Tomorrow*, pp. 38–41.

6. Eric Berne, *Games People Play*, pp. 73–81.
7. Claude Steiner, *Games Alcoholics Play* (Paperback), p. 87.
8. *Ibid.*, pp. 83–103.
9. Richard C. Bates, *How Alcoholic Patients Can Help Themselves* (Cassette tape).
10. Kellermann, *Merry-go-round Named Denial*, pp. 5–9.
11. Terence Williams, *Free to Care*, p. 7.
12. Roque Fajardo, *Helping Your Alcoholic before He or She Hits Bottom*, p. 67. © 1976 by Roque Fajardo. Used with permission of Crown Publishers.

CHAPTER IV

How the Family Can Stop the Merry-go-round

(Changing Oneself)

What benefits do family members derive from the continual games they play with the problem drinker? What is the "payoff" they seek, usually unconsciously? Each person in the family must learn the answers to these painful questions if he or she is to take positive action to break the deadly cycle of problem drinking.

For the spouse particularly, it may be extremely difficult to respond honestly, for she falls helplessly into the same destructive trap of self-delusion as the drinker. It may appear to her and to everyone around her that she receives absolutely no rewards from her distressing interactions with the drinker, but in order for a game to be successful, there must be "payoffs" for all participants.

The rewards may be subtle and emotionally unhealthy. As long as her husband continues to abuse alcohol, a wife can, for example, blame him completely for all of her failures and shortcomings. He offers her a handy scapegoat, allowing her to play the long-suffering martyr and bask in the comforting sympathy of relatives and friends. She can use him as an

45

excuse for all that she finds dissatisfying in her life and herself. "If it weren't for . . ." she laments, or sighs heavily, "Look how hard I've tried."

> "When the person's overall drinking pattern is examined in the context of the nuclear-family system, it becomes immediately apparent that there are a lot of "payoffs" for other members of the family. For instance, it is convenient to place responsibility for failure at school, for inadequate housekeeping, or for business incompetence on the drinking parent or spouse. Likewise, to justify the nonmedical use of drugs because the parent or parents use alcohol or tranquillizers."[1]

Family members must be willing to examine themselves carefully and give up the payoffs they receive. They must honestly want the drinker to stop using alcohol, even if it requires uncomfortable changes in their own behavior patterns and routines.

> Look deep inside yourself. Are you certain you want him to recover? Will you be able to stand a sober husband in the place of the quiet, unobtrusive one you have been having all these months or years? Will you be able to tolerate the nagging that he may direct at you when you insist on doing the things you do to try to help him? It is going to be one of the hardest things you have undertaken in your life. You may have to give it more thought than you imagined before trying.[2]

Do's and Don'ts

Some do's and don'ts can help family members do the right things for themselves and for the drinker. The following guidelines are gathered from various sources in the literature on alcoholism.

1. Family members must stop playing destructive games that perpetuate the drinking. Once they recognize their behavior as damaging, they must refuse to be caught further in the roles of Persecutor, Rescuer, or Patsy. They should not argue with the drinker or save and protect him from the painful consequences of his behavior. He must take

full responsibility for his actions without loved ones making excuses for him or trying to find reasons to justify his abuse of alcohol. He does not drink because of pressure on his job, or because his mother is domineering, or because his father was an alcoholic. These are simply artful excuses which he has invented to allow his drinking to continue undisturbed.

2. Family members must make a real effort to learn the facts about problem drinking. There is a wealth of information available in most communities, usually through the local A.A. chapter or an alcoholism treatment center. One can simply check the yellow pages under "alcoholism."

3. The family members should discuss their situation openly and fearlessly with someone who works in the field of alcoholism treatment and has actual experience with the problem. The treatment of alcoholism is an extremely specialized field. Most physicians, psychiatrists, and other professionals know astonishingly little about it.

4. As a family member learns the facts about the illness, she or he must explain calmly to the others the nature of the disease. Usually, the spouse is the one to discover this information, and she must tell the bewildered children why Daddy behaves as he does. Simply understanding a problem can make it far less frightening.

5. Family members must take an honest, personal inventory of their own selfish needs and the ways in which they may be unconsciously helping to maintain the problem drinking. They must determine what their "payoffs" have been and whether they are honestly willing to give them up.

6. Talking with the problem drinker about his drinking is effective only when everyone is calm and unemotional, and the drinker is sober. The best time may be when he is suffering from the pain of a hangover, or when he seems remorseful.

7. At this point, it may be a good idea to avoid the threatening word "alcoholic." A spouse should use the less frightening term "drinking problem" and suggest that both of them seek help together. She may point out that they need to "get more information" or "talk the problem over with someone else." This may be more effective than simply demanding that he "get treatment."

8. A spouse must begin to develop new interests and hobbies. She must not dwell endlessly on the drinking problem. She should do at least one small thing for herself on a regular basis, such as having her hair done, going to the movies, or something else she enjoys.

There are also several destructive behavior patterns which family members should avoid:

1. They should not protect the drinker, cover up for him, or make excuses to others for his irresponsible behavior.

2. Preaching, nagging, and lecturing will never change him. Such tactics simply give him a comfortable excuse to continue drinking.

3. Searching diligently for his hidden supply and righteously pouring the contents down the drain is an exercise in futility. He will simply buy more bottles and find caches in which to store them, adding an even heavier burden to the family budget.

4. It is hopeless to extract promises from him which he is incapable of keeping. Without outside help, the problem drinker is in no emotional (or even physical) shape to carry them out, and the broken promises lead to further guilt and anger.

5. Empty threats quickly begin to ring hollow. After a wife has announced ten times that she is leaving her husband, he knows perfectly well she has no real intention of doing so.

Ruth Maxwell, in her recent book *The Booze Battle*, offers another list of "do's and don'ts":

1. You no longer have to run from the disease. Start learning the facts about alcoholism.

2. You no longer have to blame the alcoholic. Start concentrating on your own actions — they are what will make or break you.

3. You no longer have to control the alcoholic's drinking. Start concentrating on his need for treatment and start offering treatment.

4. You no longer have to rescue the alcoholic. Start letting him suffer and assume responsibility for each and every consequence of his drinking.

5. You no longer have to be concerned with the alcoholic's reasons for drinking. Start resuming a normal living pattern.

6. You no longer have to threaten. Start saying what you mean and doing what you say.

7. You no longer have to accept or extract promises. Start rejecting them.

8. You no longer have to seek advice from the uninformed. Start your commitment to treatment and long-range goals of health.

9. You no longer have to hide the fact that you are seeking help. Start telling the alcoholic that you are.

10. You no longer have to nag, preach, coax, and lecture. Start reporting his inappropriate actions to him.

11. You no longer have to allow the alcoholic to assault you or your children. Start protecting yourself.

12. You no longer have to be a puppet. Start detaching yourself.[3]

Five Suggestions

The wife cannot solve the drinker's problem by worrying continually about him. She must learn to think about herself and her children. The following five suggestions will help her accomplish this goal:

1. She should join Al-Anon.

2. She should get the children to Alateen.

3. She should avoid getting caught up in the "whys" of problem drinking.

4. She should learn how her own emotions work and how she can change them.

5. She should learn the "how's" and "when's" of a helpful *crisis.*

This chapter will discuss the first four of these suggestions in considerable detail. Number five is the subject of the following chapter.

Joining Al-Anon

Al-Anon is a fellowship of spouses, relatives, and friends of problem drinkers. They try to solve their common problems by sharing their knowledge and experience. The following twelve steps are the foundation of Al-Anon.

1. We admitted we were powerless over alcohol — that our lives had become unmanageable.

2. Came to believe that a Power greater than ourselves could restore us to sanity.

3. Made a decision to turn our will and our lives over to the care of God *as we understood Him.*

4. Made a searching and fearless moral inventory of ourselves.

5. Admitted to God, to ourselves and to another human being the exact nature of our wrongs.

6. Were entirely ready to have God remove all these defects of character.

7. Humbly asked Him to remove our shortcomings.

8. Made a list of all persons we had harmed and became willing to make amends to them all.

9. Made direct amends to such people wherever possible except when to do so would injure them or others.

10. Continued to take personal inventory and when we were wrong, promptly admitted it.

11. Sought through prayer and meditation to improve our conscious contact with God as we understood Him, praying only for knowledge of His will for us and the power to carry that out.

12. Having had a spiritual awakening as the result of these Steps, we tried to carry this message to others, and to practice these principles in all our affairs.[4]

By understanding and applying these principles in their own lives, one day at a time, Al-Anon members learn constructive ways of dealing with the problem drinker within their individual family systems. They quit reacting to him and begin to think about their own problems.

What else can Al-Anon do for the bewildered spouse or friend of the problem drinker? Al-Anon literature expresses clearly the answer to this question:

What Al-Anon Can Do for You

The following quotation from Al-Anon literature explains how Al-Anon can help.

- It can build up your own confidence and serenity, which in turn can help the alcoholic to want sobriety.

- Your improved attitude can help your husband or wife embrace sobriety with an easy mind; enjoyed sobriety is the kind that lasts!

- It can help you to create a normal environment for your children, the most dependable defense against their becoming neurotic, delinquent, or alcoholic.

- It can improve your general health, physically by removing the cause of nervousness, mentally by conquering fear, worry and anxiety, and spiritually through providing you with the means of gaining humility, peace of mind, and a living faith.[5]

There are two vital truths (expressed in a total of seven

words) which a newcomer learns when she or he first comes to Al-Anon. They provide the basis for all the constructive action that she or he can later learn and apply to his or her own life. These truths are simply: 1) *he is sick*, and 2) *I am not responsible.*

A wife must be careful to remember that she comes to Al-Anon to help herself, not to stop her husband from drinking. She is powerless over his problem. A change in his behavior may be the happy outcome of the alterations she and other family members make in themselves, but this hope should not be the reason for joining Al-Anon. A person goes to Al-Anon to help herself (or himself).

Alateen

A spouse who is trying to deal effectively with a drinking problem in the family should supply her children with literature and encourage them to attend Alateen. Alateen is an outgrowth of Al-Anon and is especially for the teen-aged sons and daughters of the problem drinker. By learning and following the same twelve steps of A.A. and Al-Anon, the Alateen member develops positive ways to deal with the drinking in the family system.

If the children in a family have any doubt that they need Alateen, they should answer the following questions for themselves.

- Do you have a parent, close friend or relative with a drinking problem?
- Do you feel you got a rotten break in life?
- Do you hate one or both of your parents?
- Have you lost respect for your non-alcoholic parent?
- Do you try to get even with your parents when you think they have been unfair?
- Are you ashamed of your home?
- Do you wish your home could be more like the homes of your friends?

- Do you lose your temper a lot?
- Do you sometimes say and do things you don't want to do, but can't help it?
- Do you have trouble concentrating on school work?
- Do you resent having to do jobs around the house that you think your parents should be doing?
- Are you afraid to let people know what you're really like?
- Do you sometimes wish you were dead?
- Are you starting to think it would be nice to forget your problems by taking drugs or getting drunk?
- Is it hard for you to talk to your parents? Do you talk to them at all?
- Do you go to extremes to get people to like you?
- Are you afraid of the future?
- Do you believe no one could possibly understand how you feel?
- Do you feel you make your alcoholic parent drink?
- Do you get upset when your parents fight?
- Do you stay out of the house as much as possible because you hate it there?
- Do you avoid telling your parents the truth?
- Do you worry about your parents?
- Are you nervous or scared a lot of the time?
- Do you resent the alcoholic's drinking?
- Do you feel nobody really loves you or cares what happens to you?
- Do you feel like a burden to your parents?
- Do you sometimes do freaky or way out things to get attention?
- Do you cover up your real feelings by pretending you don't care?
- Do you take advantage of your parents when you know you can get away with it?[6]

If a child answers "yes" to some of the above questions and is close to someone with a drinking problem, Alateen can offer the vital help he or she needs.

The "Why's"

One of the most normal and natural things that people do is to look for the *cause* (the why) of things that happen. For the loved ones of a problem drinker, this search usually takes the form of a series of futile questions: "*Why* does he drink?" "*Why* is he doing this to us?" They harbor the erroneous belief that if they knew *why* he behaves as he does, his drinking would cease automatically. The fact is that the cause is unimportant, and the constant, fruitless search for it takes the focus off the vital work of solving the problem. The time that one wastes analyzing the possibilities is time that could be spent on doing something about the problem. Becoming preoccupied with "why" the problem exists is disheartening and self-defeating.

Melville Gooderham, a physician at the Addiction Research Foundation in Toronto, Canada, speaks to this point succinctly:

> How the pattern started is relatively unimportant. Instead of searching for the "Holy Grail" or "cause," long since buried in history, attention should be directed toward determining what is maintaining the on-going, dysfunctional behavior pattern, or, "What are the payoffs for the problem drinker, for the individual members of his family, and for the nuclear-family-system-as-a-whole that maintains the pathological drinking behavior on his part?"[7]

The Wegschieders suggest, "Looking back into the system and into what caused the alcoholism is academic and not necessary for recovery. We work with what is. We work with the current system."[8]

This is a very important insight, because so many people seem to lose their way in a fruitless search for "why's." It does not matter *why*. When an orthopedic surgeon sees someone with a broken leg in the emergency room, it makes little difference to him whether the victim injured himself in a fall, with a baseball bat, or in a soccer game. Regardless of the cause, the treatment is the same. In the same way, when problem drinking injures the family system, the cause does not matter. What does matter is that the other family members increase their knowledge of problem drinking, become aware of what they are doing to maintain it, and determine that they will initiate changes which will help them. These are the best ways they can help the problem drinker.

Emotions — How They Work

Perhaps the most helpful thing that the spouse of a problem drinker can do is to learn about her own feelings of worry, anger, anxiety, guilt, nervousness, fear, frustration, and depression. All human beings feel these emotions at times, but the family of a problem drinker suffers more frequently and acutely from them than others do.

Where do these feelings come from? What causes a person to become upset? The spouse of a problem drinker would probably answer quickly, "His drinking, of course."

She may firmly believe this is true, and her friends may insist sympathetically that she is right, but the truth is that there is no way another person or event can make someone feel angry, fearful, depressed, or worthless. One does these things entirely to oneself.

The spouse makes countless statements such as:

"He came home drunk and made me so angry . . ."
"He makes me feel so guilty . . ."
"He causes me to worry so much that . . ."
"He makes me so nervous when . . ."
"He upsets me whenever . . ."

In reality, however, "he," "she," or "it," does not upset anyone. A wife creates these undesirable feelings herself, and she alone can change them. Serenity and happiness do not depend upon the behavior of others. They come from within oneself.

The Rational Counseling Model

An ABC model offers a helpful framework for understanding the beginning of emotions. Before a person experiences an emotion (C), he or she goes through two preliminary steps (A and B) which lead to the feeling.

A. First, there is an activating event, situation, or perception (something one sees, hears, smells, tastes, or touches).

B. Second, one thinks about or evaluates the event.

C. Third, in response to the thought, there comes an emotional reaction.

Human beings experience these steps continually. The following examples illustrate how they work in everyday life:

"Suppose you are on a crowded elevator and someone behind you starts poking you with an object. Being unable to turn around and protest, let's assume that like most people, you begin to get angry and upset. As the elevator lets you off on your floor you decide to give this person a piece of your mind. Just as you are about to begin, you suddenly realize the person is blind, and quite unknowingly poking you with his cane.

"What happens to your anger? To your proposed tongue-lashing? Well, it's difficult to speak for everyone, but probably many people would get much less upset. They might even replace their hostile feelings with pity, and some might even feel guilty and upset with themselves for almost criticizing a handicapped person.

"What caused the drastic change in feelings in the example? Very simply, new ideas or attitudes resulting from looking at the situation differently. In other words, a change in mind caused a change in feelings."[9]

A second example might be a boy who is walking in the

woods and sees a snake (Part A). He becomes frightened and runs away. Later, he tells his friend about what happened. "I saw a big snake and it really scared me," he exclaims. The snake itself, however, did not frighten the boy. His own thoughts about snakes (Part B) made him feel scared. He may have told himself, "It's going to bite me. It's poisonous. Snakes are slimy, ugly creatures."

Some other walker might react in an entirely different way to the snake. He or she might think, "Snakes are good pets," or "I love to play with them." He or she might even be extremely happy to have had the good fortune to have spotted the creature.

It is not, then, other people or things in themselves which cause emotions. The thoughts a person has about an event or situation create his or her feelings.

A third example of the ABC sequence is a woman driving to an important appointment. She is not yet late, but she has no time to waste and is driving a bit faster than usual.

Suddenly she hears a siren, and looking through her rear-view mirror, she sees the flashing red light of a police car behind her. (This is Part A, the actual event.) She fumes to herself, "Of all times for the police to stop me. That cop was probably sitting there waiting. He should be spending his time searching for real criminals." (This is Part B, her evaluation of the situation.) She becomes extremely upset and angry (Part C).

As she begins to pull over, the police car overtakes her and keeps going. She experiences a quick change in her thinking and sighs, "Well, he wasn't after me at all. I'm safe. I didn't *think* I deserved a ticket."

Most people would insist that it was the police car that frightened the woman and made her angry, but the truth of the matter is that the fear resulted from the way she interpreted the situation. People learn to believe certain things about particular situations, and these rigid thoughts cause them to feel the way they do. Thus, a change in attitude can result in a corresponding change in emotion.

Point A (facts and events) does not cause Point C (feelings). Point B (thoughts and beliefs) is directly responsible for the emotions a person experiences. Thus, irrational attitudes, self-defeating beliefs, and false assumptions can result in a needless struggle with painful emotions. This is the basic principle of rational counseling. As the Greek philosopher, Epictetus, declared, "Men are disturbed not by things themselves, but what they think of things." Shakespeare put it another way, "There is nothing bad nor good, but thinking makes it so," and the French philosopher, Montaigne, conveyed the same idea when he said, "A man is hurt not so much by what happens, as by his opinion of what happens."

Rational counseling offers new hope to people who carry a burden of negative emotions. The method teaches them to challenge and dispute irrational, unrealistic ideas and replace them with reasonable, sensible ones. Renowned psychologist Albert Ellis, from the Institute of Rational Living in New York, lists ten common self-defeating attitudes which cause unnecessary pain and frustration for the person who believes them.

1. *The idea that you must — yes, must — have love or approval from all the people you find significant.*
2. *The idea that you must prove thoroughly competent, adequate, and achieving or a saner but still foolish variation: The idea that you must have competence or talent in some important area.*
3. *The idea that when people act obnoxiously and unfairly, you should blame and damn them, and see them as bad, wicked, or rotten individuals.*
4. *The idea that you have to view things as awful, terrible, horrible, and catastrophic when you get seriously frustrated, treated unfairly, or rejected.*
5. *The idea that emotional misery comes from external pressures and that you have little ability to control or change your feelings.*
6. *The idea that if something seems dangerous or fearsome, you must preoccupy yourself with and make yourself anxious about it.*
7. *The idea that you can more easily avoid facing many of life's*

    difficulties and self-responsibilities than undertake more reward-
ing forms of self-discipline.
8. *The idea that your past remains all important and that because*
something once strongly influenced your life, it has to keep deter-
mining your feelings and behavior today.
9. *The idea that people and things should turn out better than they*
do and that you must view it as awful and horrible if you do not
find good solutions to life's grim realities.
10. *The idea that you can achieve maximum human happiness by*
inertia and inaction or by passively and uncommittedly "enjoying
yourself." [10]

Perhaps the two most common words found in these irrational attitudes are "should" and "awful." A careful examination of them reveals that they are the cause of a great number
of needless problems.

Should's

The word "should" is harmless and rational when it refers
to probability. It is completely rational, for example, to point
out that, "If a light bulb drops on the sidewalk, it *should*
break." Such a statement is simply a scientific confirmation of
the physical nature of events — "If one does this, that most
likely will follow."

When a person uses absolutes such as "should," "ought," or
"must" to make an unreasonable demand of himself or someone else, however, he exhibits an attitude which is bound to
plunge him into trouble. If he insists that he or other people
be different in some way, anger and frustration will quickly
follow. A person cannot change reality, or the way things are,
no matter how desperately he wants things to be the way he
likes them to be. It is foolish, for example, to stare out the
window and complain, "It shouldn't be raining today — I had
a golf date." It *is* raining, and no amount of wishing will
disperse the clouds. By insisting that it should *not* be raining,
one invites anger and distress.

Why, after all, should things happen exactly as one wishes?
Who said they "should"? Life becomes much easier if one

begins to think in this way: "I don't *like* the fact that it's raining. I wish it were sunny, but I don't always get what I want. I can't change the facts, so there is no use getting upset."

Awful's

Words in the "awful" category lead every bit as speedily to negative feelings as do "should's." Phrases such as, "It's awful," "I can't stand it," and "What a terrible thing," can quickly transform unfortunate, disappointing events into complete disasters.

Exaggerations such as "awful" and "dreadful" are irrational because no objective evidence exists to indicate that anyone or anything is "awful" or "dreadful." Thinking or believing something is unbearable, however, leads inevitably to unpleasant emotions.

Healthy feelings are the result of continually disputing words that suggest catastrophe by asking "Why? Why is it awful? Where is proof that anything is so terrible?"

"Should's" and "awful's" create an enormous number of bad feelings. By applying rational counseling techniques, a person can completely change his feelings about a situation, resulting in a new freedom from negative emotions. The following example shows how the family can apply these techniques to the struggle of living with a problem drinker.

Perhaps the drinker staggers in late at night and, in his drunken state, begins to criticize and shout at his wife. She becomes extremely angry and screams back at him. What can she do differently to change this disturbing scene the next time it happens?

She must remember first that the problem drinker uses her anger selfishly to rationalize future alcohol abuse. If she can change the way she thinks so he fails to arouse her anger, he will no longer have this important weapon at his disposal.

A wife might begin the difficult process of changing her thinking by writing down all the disturbing thoughts she had when her husband barged into the house and began to criticize her. She might include such phrases as, "He shouldn't do this," "I can't stand it," "He's an awful person," "This is dreadful," or "If he really loved me and the children he wouldn't. . . ."

Next, she should critically examine her thoughts to see if they are rational and begin to replace nonsensical ideas with sensible ones. Instead of insisting irrationally, "He shouldn't do this," she should tell herself calmly, "I don't like what he is doing, but getting myself angry over it is not going to change the fact that he is doing it. I know that I have no control over how he behaves, and it is foolish to get upset about something over which I am powerless. I will choose a good time, maybe tomorrow when he's sober, and explain to him how I feel about his behavior. Then, if he continues to act this way, I can choose to leave him. I don't like the idea, but I may make that choice. Things will be difficult for awhile for me and the children, but we'll survive. Living without him would be far better than continuing in this unbearable drinking situation."

If the spouse of a problem drinker learns and practices rational counseling, she will become calmer and happier. The process is difficult, and she will never achieve her goal by simply pretending that she is not angry. She must work hard at practicing positive thoughts which cause better feelings. Gradually, she will find that she does not get nearly so upset and that she becomes disturbed far less frequently.

In summary, some of the benefits the spouse of a problem drinker can derive from practicing rational counseling include:

1. A continuing realization that she cannot control the behavior of the drinker or any other person. She can change only herself.

2. The ability to be calm and happy even while the problem drinking continues. Being calm and rational means she will be in a better position to make a correct decision about what to do if he fails to stop drinking.

3. The ability to refuse to allow the drinker to justify further

alcohol abuse by arousing her anxiety and anger. She must stop playing her part in the game.

The comforting serenity Prayer, which one learns in Al-Anon, embodies beautifully all the ideas of rational counseling in four succinct lines:

> God grant me the serenity
> To accept the things I cannot change
> Courage to change the things I can,
> And the wisdom to know the difference.

Rational self-counseling offers the wife of a problem drinker the tools to change the things she can — her emotional reactions to his drinking. The next chapter makes other suggestions for taking positive action to intervene in the downward spiral of alcohol abuse.

NOTES

Chapter IV

1. Melville Gooderham, "The Therapy of Relationships," *Addictions*, p. 61.
2. Roque Fajardo, *Helping Your Alcoholic before He or She Hits Bottom*, p. 67. © 1976 by Roque Fajardo. Used with permission of Crown Publishers.
3. Ruth Maxwell, *The Booze Battle*, pp. 191–192. © 1976 by Praeger Publishers, Inc. Reprinted with permission of Holt, Rinehart and Winston.
4. *This Is Al-Anon*, pp. 4–5.
5. *This is Al-Anon*, p. 9.
6. *Alateen: Hope for the Children of Alcoholics*, pp. 1–2.
7. Gooderham, "The Therapy of Relationships," p. 62.
8. Don and Sharon Wegscheider, *Family Illness: Chemical Dependency*, p. 8.
9. Howard S. Young, *A Rational Counseling Primer*, p. 10.
10. Albert Ellis and Robert A. Harper, *A New Guide to Rational Living* (paperback), pp. 88–195.

CHAPTER V

How the Family Can Intervene

(The Family Acts, and the Drinker Must Change)

Chapter I presented the basic concept and the general laws of a system. It explained that when one part or member of a system changes, the rest of the system must change as well. This is the key principle which makes it possible for the family to intervene in the problem drinking behavior.

Unless family members realize that changing their own actions often results in a corresponding positive change in the drinker, they will assume they are helpless victims who must wait patiently until he asks for help. "He has to hit rock-bottom first," runs the old cliché. This is simply not true. The belief is a dangerous myth which results in needless unhappiness for everyone.

A look at occupational programs illustrates the fallacy of this belief. Employee Assistance Programs, or "Troubled Employee Programs," as they are sometimes called, often boast very high improvement rates. These vital programs do not work if the persons involved wait quietly until the drinker asks for help. The drinker's supervisor documents carefully all objective evidence of deteriorating work performance.

When he gathers enough information, he confronts the employee and offers him the choice of accepting help or losing his job.

Positive Intervention

Families, as well as employers, are in an excellent position to intervene in the deadly cycle of problem drinking and force an "earlier bottom" for the drinker. They can help him reach a crisis sooner than he would otherwise, perhaps before he has sunk into the final, life-threatening stages of the illness.

The spouse can begin the life-saving process of family intervention by changing her reactions to the drinking. When she changes her responses, she forces him to change his behavior as well.

> If one partner makes a change, the other partner must accommodate to that change with changes of his own to balance the relationship, else it ceases to exist. That's the nature of relationships. With help from outside the whirlpool, either partner can stop the destruction for himself. When he does, his partner is going to have to accommodate to that change to restore the balance of the relationship, or it will cease to exist. Either way, the partner reaching outside the whirlpool of alcoholism for help cannot lose. At the very least, she stops her own destruction, at the most, she makes it possible for her partner to stop his as well. In alcoholic marriages, it is only when one of the partners reaches out that both can be helped. When one of them starts to replace negative actions with positive actions, the climate is set for constructive changes in the other partner. *Every positive change made by the partner reaching for help contains the potential for positive responses from the other.*[1]

Family members can make constructive changes which will certainly help them and may cause the problem drinker to realize he needs treatment. They can also carry the process one step further and intervene directly in a way that increases tremendously the chances of creating a crisis which will force him to seek help. The systems theory explains why it is possible to intervene and cause changes in the behavior of another person. The rest of this chapter will focus on how and when to do it successfully.

Intervention Techniques

Family members can intervene successfully in two ways:

1. *They can refuse to do anything which will prevent a drinking crisis.* The spouse especially must realize that sheltering the drinker from the consequences of his behavior is not really a kindness. While it saves temporary embarrassment, it destroys a potential source of motivation for change. She must stop covering his bad checks and paying the bills at the liquor store. When he is too sick to go to work, she must refuse to make excuses to his boss. Left unprotected, the drinker becomes much more vulnerable to active intervention.

2. *They can learn how to create a confrontation.* A confrontation can take various forms, but the family must manufacture some kind of "bottom," or crisis, which will bring the drinker to the painful realization that he cannot continue as he has been. Jim McWilliams, a family counselor at the Kansas City Area National Council on Alcoholism, offers the following method of dealing with this difficult problem.

A Suggested Method of Confronting the Alcoholic

(This should be done when the drinker is sober enough to understand.)

_____, I have something very important to discuss with you and I want you to hear me through. There should be no question about whether I love you or not, but just in case there is, I want to assure you that I do love you — I love you very much. But I have been sitting idly by, watching you slowly but surely destroying yourself, and us with you, and I didn't know what to do.

So I went down to the National Council on Alcoholism to find out what I could do, and this is what they told me.

After describing your drinking pattern, they pointed out to me that *your drinking is not social drinking* by any stretch of the imagination — *your kind of drinking is sick* and will get even sicker — but there is help for you if you want it, and I hope you get it. They also told me that DRINKING IS YOUR PROBLEM and there is nothing I can do about it — nor can anyone else, not even your employer. He can fire you, but he can't make you stop drinking — so I am not even going to try anymore.

HOWEVER, they told me that I, too, have a problem — separate and distinct from your problem, even though they are interrelated. *MY* problem is *my feeling about your drinking and your behavior*, plus *my reaction to it — it is making me sick*. Now, they tell me that while I can do nothing about your problem, there is plenty I can do about mine, and I'm going to do it!

At their suggestion, I am getting into Al-Anon — NOT FOR YOU, BUT FOR ME. I hope to find out what is wrong with me and correct it. But most of all I am going there to get confidence, self-assurance, and courage so that I can make a life for myself (and the children) with or without you. I hope it is with you, _____, but in any event, they tell me that I need never let your drinking make me sick again — and I don't intend to! NOTE: (UNDERSTAND, WE ARE NOT TALKING ABOUT DIVORCE OR SEPARATION — NOT AT THIS POINT, ANYWAY.)

By the way, _____, I am never, ever going to have a drink with you again, nor will I go anywhere with you when you have had *even one drink* or when you are going to have *even one drink* — not that I am opposed to drinking — in fact, I may have a drink from time to time with the girls, but never again with you, because your kind of drinking is sick and suicidal and I will have no part of it.

Note: (You must be willing to follow through completely and persistently or this will not work. Don't start it unless you intend to follow through. Another and most important warning: this creation of a crisis — or confrontation — must be done out of a motive of love and not out of resentment or retaliation or to satisfy your anger.)

When There Are Children in the Home

Oh, yes, _____, there is a third problem they mentioned. Do you realize, _____, that you and I have been playing a silly, childish game with each other at the expense of our children? Do you realize that you and I are making the children sick? Now I don't know what you intend to do about it, but I am dropping out of this silly game, so there won't be any more games, and I am going to sit the children down and explain to them just exactly what the problem is.

Oh, don't worry, _____, I am not going to "knock" you or belittle you — quite the contrary, I want to build you up in their eyes. I want them to love and respect you — they need to even if you don't care.

I am going to explain to them that their father is not an evil man or a thoughtless man — he is a very good man and he loves us, but he is also very, very sick — he is suffering from the effects of alcohol, and he doesn't really know how sick he is. So, children, if you see your mother doing some things that you think are harsh or cruel, understand I am not doing them to get even with your father — quite the contrary, I will be doing them because I love him and want to save his life.

(Then you *do* sit the children down and tell them this. If you have children who are in their teens, by all means see that they get into an Alateen group.)[2]

Roque Fajardo, founder of Samaritan Center in Nashville, Tennessee, suggests a series of five steps which the wife may use in the process of confrontation (guided intervention).

Step 1

The first thing the wife must do is create a quiet, calm atmosphere in the home. She must refrain from fussing, nag-

ging, threatening, or engaging in any of the ineffective behaviors mentioned in Chapter IV. In Step 1, called the
"feather touch," she simply announces calmly to the drinker
that she is going to do something constructive about *her* problem, such as attending an A.A. meeting or going to a counselor. She should invite him to come along, but she should not
try to persuade or force him. At this point, she puts no
pressure at all on him, but continues to attend meetings or
sessions faithfully, whether or not he accompanies her. Before she leaves and after she returns home from a meeting,
she reports her activities briefly and unemotionally to him
and then refrains from mentioning the meeting or session
again. If he resists her efforts or tries to convince her to quit
attending meetings or seeing her counselor, she must refuse
to allow herself to argue with him. Even if he stops drinking
temporarily, she must continue with the vital process of getting help for herself.

Step 2

It is not unusual for the drinker to fail to respond to these
gentle announcements and invitations. In Step 2, the wife
insists that he accompany her to meetings or counseling sessions. She refrains from making threats or delivering an ul-
timatum, giving him time to make up his own mind. She and
the counselor decide together how long she should wait before proceeding to the next step.

Step 3

If the drinker continues to refuse to take positive action to
deal with his problem, his wife delivers a short but meaning-
ful speech, stating firmly that if he does not begin attending
sessions or meetings by a certain deadline, she will have to try
something else. She may, perhaps, ask her counselor to come
to the house and speak frankly with her husband (doorbell
intervention). When the counselor arrives, the house should
be quiet and she should be at home, but out of the way,

perhaps in the back yard, so the drinker and the counselor can talk privately.

Step 4

If doorbell intervention fails, the wife may try the quasi-legal approach. She declares again that her husband must seek help, telling him determinedly that if he has done nothing by a certain deadline, she will see a lawyer. She then seeks out a competent lawyer who understands clearly that her goal at this point is not a divorce. She simply wants desperately to force her husband to accept help. The lawyer sends the drinker a letter requesting him to begin (or resume) attending sessions or meetings. He mentions no other legal action, but if the drinker still refuses obstinately to do anything constructive, the lawyer sends a follow-up letter setting a firm deadline.

Step 5

When a wife follows these steps faithfully, the problem drinker will usually break the destructive pattern of problem drinking by responding finally to help. In some particularly difficult cases, however, a temporary separation may be necessary to jolt him out of the alcoholic haze enveloping him. The wife insists firmly that he must move out, or under some circumstances, she herself may leave. She assures him of her continuing love, offering him a clear choice of keeping her by seeking treatment or destroying the marriage by continuing to drink.

Even if he responds at last and begins attending meetings, the wife should wait patiently for at least a month before she considers a reunion, making certain that during this time he is trying honestly to deal constructively with his problem. It is important for her to continue faithfully with her Al-Anon meetings and/or professional counseling.[3]

The Johnson Institute has developed a specific method of family intervention designed to get the drinker to accept as quickly as possible the lifesaving treatment he needs. Professional help may be necessary for carrying out the program.

1. The family first organizes an intervention team, consisting of two or more persons who have witnessed the destructive behavior of the problem drinker. It is possible for only one person to intervene, but two or more have a vastly greater impact. Beloved friends, esteemed co-workers, and the employer can be important members of the team. Children who have suffered from the behavior of the drinker are often extremely effective in forcing him to see himself realistically.

2. Each member of the team prepares a detailed written list of specific incidents involving alcohol abuse which he or she has witnessed personally. Dealing with actual events forces the drinker to acknowledge that their concern about his problem is legitimate. Family members should conscientiously avoid opinions and generalized statements such as:

    "You're always drinking"
    "You drink too much"
    "Your drinking is getting worse"
    "You might get fired."

    They should point out instead:

    "Last week I found another empty bottle in your bureau drawer"
    "In the past two years, you've had two drunk driving charges"
    "Last Saturday night you fell down in the bathroom at two a.m."
    "That same night you came home slurring your words, accused me of infidelity, and knocked over the lamp in the living room."

3. Team members should agree upon the various alternatives they will offer the drinker when they confront him.

4. Team members must anticipate the many excuses and alibis the drinker will give to justify his refusal to accept the choices they offer him. They should carefully prepare irrefutable answers in advance. Some excuses he may present are:

"I can't get off work to go to treatment"

"Treatment is expensive. We can't afford it."

"Our health insurance won't cover it."

5. The team must agree to insist on a "what if" clause in case the drinker rejects completely all their alternatives by declaring, "I can do it myself. I'm simply not going to drink again." If this happens, the family must persuade the drinker to agree to enter treatment if his own attempts at recovery prove futile. It must be firmly understood that even one drink constitutes failure on his part.

6. The next step is choosing a team chairman who will have the responsibility of stating calmly the purpose of the meeting, selecting the order of presentations, offering the choice of alternatives, and summarizing the concerns of the team.

7. The team must then set a date for the vital confrontation. An ideal time is when they can take the drinker by surprise, perhaps while he is suffering from a severe hangover and his defenses are low.

8. During the confrontation, team members must carefully avoid allowing the drinker to play one of them off against another. They should adhere closely to their written lists of incidents and remain calm and objective while they voice their concern for him. They must be firm and specific and refuse to argue or become defensive.[4]

Questions about Intervention

Family members may have many troubling questions about the intervention process. The Johnson Institute offers the following answers to some of the more common ones:

Do I have a right to interfere?

Alcoholism is a fatal disease. If the alcoholic continues to drink, he will inevitably die prematurely. You not only have the right, you have the responsibility to intervene in a disease of this magnitude. To do so effectively, however, you must truly care about the person and what happens to him. If you act out of love and concern, you are not interfering.

How do I help when no one else seems to care?

You will often discover that there are others who do care, but they are so frightened and baffled by the disease they are afraid to come forward. Educating these people can be an important step toward positive intervention. If you find you are indeed the only person who cares enough to take action, that is all the more reason for you to assume the responsibility to do your best to help the sick person.

Will he hate me forever?

One of the defenses that the alcoholic uses skillfully is anger, so it is not unusual to encounter hostility when you are trying desperately to intervene. At this point, hostility is a symptom of the disease. When the drinker gets well, he will certainly not hate you but will be exceedingly grateful that you cared enough to save his very life.

What do I do if he doesn't want help?

The alcoholic deludes himself into believing he is not sick and does not need treatment. This denial is a symptom of the disease. The intervention process is designed specifically to break through the alcoholic fog of delusions and force him to see that he needs help desperately.

What if the intervention process fails?

Intervention is not always successful the first time. Its effects are cumulative, however, and it is extremely unlikely that attempting to intervene will cause any harm. The only danger lies in the redoubled efforts he may make to hide his problem more effectively. Even an unsuccessful attempt at intervention makes the drinker more aware of his problem and may result in an easier intervention later.[5]

The family, especially the spouse, is in an excellent position to take the initiative in planning the intervention strategy. All family members can learn to take positive action which will help them and will create a crisis for the problem drinker. By continuing constructive confrontation, the family increases tremendously the probability that the drinker will decide to seek treatment.

As Ruth Maxwell states,

> Today, thousands of wives are learning how to approach their alcoholic husbands differently. They are stopping the old actions which abetted their husbands' drinking, and which increased their own misery. They are substituting new actions which make it increasingly difficult for their husbands to continue drinking. In the process, the wives are regaining their sense of self-worth and their freedom. They are no longer puppets to their alcoholic husbands, therefore, their husbands are forced to change; many are getting sober.[6]

The family cannot stop the problem drinker from destroying himself, but by using positive intervention techniques, they can greatly increase his chances of getting into treatment.

The essence of the intervention process is caught in the words of psychiatrist R. D. Laing:

There must be something the matter with him
    because he would not be acting as he does
    unless there was
    therefore he is acting the way he is
    because there is something the matter with him

He does not think there is anything the matter
    with him because
        one of the things that is
        the matter with him
        is that he does not think there is anything
            the matter with him

Therefore
        We have to help him realize that
        the fact that he does not think there is anything
        the matter with him
        is one of the things that is
            the matter with him [7]

R. D. Laing

NOTES

Chapter V

1. Ruth Maxwell, *The Booze Battle*, p. 161. © 1976 by Praeger Publishers, Inc. Reprinted by permission of Holt, Rinehart and Winston.
2. Jim McWilliams, 1977: personal communication. (Jim McWilliams works with the Kansas City Area National Council on Alcoholism.)
3. Roque Fajardo, *Helping Your Alcoholic before He or She Hits Bottom*, pp. 90–108. © 1976 by Roque Fajardo. Used by permission of Crown Publishers.
4. *Intervention*. Johnson Institute.
5. *I'll Quit Tomorrow* (Training manual for film), pp. 11–12.
6. Maxwell, *Booze Battle*, p. 57. © 1976 by Praeger Publishers, Inc. Reprinted by permission of Holt, Rinehart and Winston.
7. R. D. Laing, untitled poem in *The Booze Battle* by Ruth Maxwell, p. xiv. © 1976 by Praeger Publishers, Inc. Reprinted by permission of Holt, Rinehart and Winston.

CHAPTER VI

The Family System in Treatment

(What Changes Are Necessary?)

It is tragic when the problem drinker fails to get help, but it is just as tragic if he enters treatment while the rest of the family refuses to deal positively with their own difficulties. By the time problem drinking has reached the middle and later stages, the condition of each family member has deteriorated drastically to the point where it is almost impossible to recover from the devastating effects of the disease without outside help.

The drinker himself suffers from complete self-delusion. He has created a highly structured defense system which utterly distorts his view of reality. He is totally out of touch with himself and his feelings.

The other family members have developed distressingly poor self-concepts and suffer from an alarming lack of self-esteem. To a great extent, they have lost their individual identities and are brimming with negative feelings such as anger, resentment, and self-pity. The destructive, self-defeating ways they have learned to deal with the drinker and each other are the only weapons they have to help them in their painful struggle.

The Wegscheiders express it thus:

All family members are out of touch with their power to generate good feelings for themselves.

All family members feel powerless to change the situation.

All family members carry this dysfunction with them as part of their personality pattern, and one of two things happens.

1. The dysfunctional traits tend to interfere in their outside lives or,
2. They develop two personalities, one for the family and one for school and friends.

Either way, it's an escape from being what they really are feeling.[1]

While the problem drinker is abusing alcohol, the entire family system suffers from severe strain and fragmentation. Roles and relationships become painfully distorted. Responsibilities switch from one person to another and communication breaks down disturbingly. The system loses its equilibrium and becomes totally out of balance. The family is "dis-eased."

If the problem drinker goes into treatment alone, he returns afterwards to a family system that is still dysfunctional. The other family members remain locked into the compulsive behavior patterns they acquired while the drinker was abusing alcohol. Since they have learned nothing about the problem nor explored their own needs and feelings, a tremendous amount of stress still exists within the family system. When the drinker returns from treatment, no one will know how to act or react, so they will feel constantly as if they were "walking on eggshells."

Thus, if the family system is to regain its vigor and health, every member must receive the vital treatment necessary for recovery. Treatment helps to diffuse the destructive fear, guilt, anxiety, and resentment that will otherwise result in a future explosion.

An Additional Value of Family Therapy

Treating the entire family also helps to point out that the drinker is not a bad person who has deliberately harmed those he loves. He is simply one member of a sick family system which needs help desperately. The entire family becomes "the patient," not just one person.

Margaret Cork says, "Family therapy is not a matter of using family members as an adjunct to the alcoholic's treatment; it is, rather, a process of helping all members to deal with their own conflicts, emotional upsets, and difficulties in interpersonal relationships."[2]

All too often, family members fail tragically to get into treatment along with the problem drinker. There are usually two reasons for this. First, the family feels a sudden, welcome relief that the drinker is away for awhile. They want to forget their troubles and enjoy blissful peace and quiet for a few weeks. The second reason is far less excusable: few treatment centers bother to solicit the participation of the family. Even fewer have special programs designed to deal particularly with the needs of other family members.

Even if the problem drinker refuses to seek help, it is vital for the rest of the family to become involved in treatment. They can benefit enormously by learning what they are doing to prolong the drinking and by exploring intervention techniques and the options which are open to them. In some cases, the wife will reach the painful decision that separation or divorce offers the only alternative.

Often, however, when the family changes its destructive behavior patterns, the drinker does seek treatment. The planned intervention approach of the Johnson Institute is successful 70 percent of the time. When the drinker reaches out for help and enters a treatment program, the other family members need to work diligently on their own problems.

Choosing the Right Program

The drinker and the family may choose an inpatient or

outpatient program, depending upon circumstances. Inpatient programs have the advantage of a period of concentrated and intensive treatment, giving the drinker and family members a chance to focus completely on recovery.

It is vital to choose a treatment facility that offers a special program for the family and encourages participation in A.A., Al-Anon, and Alateen. The family should be certain to select a facility specializing in the treatment of alcoholism and to avoid those that are primarily psychiatric hospitals. Less than 10 percent of problem drinkers need psychiatric care.

The drinker and his family need to learn and experience several important things during the treatment process. Perhaps the most vital for the drinker is the breakdown of his elaborate denial system. He learns that he has an illness and accepts that it will always be a part of his life. He admits he is powerless over alcohol and that his life has become unmanageable. This opens him to a new freedom to develop fresh attitudes and learn to accept responsibility for his behavior and his life. He discovers healthy new ways to deal with his problems and feelings without the use of mood-altering chemicals.

The other members of the family system have learned gradually to deal with the drinking in compulsive, nonproductive ways. They bring these destructive behavior patterns with them to treatment, as well as their disturbing feelings of low self-esteem and self-defeating attitudes. Treatment offers them a unique opportunity to get in touch with the anger, guilt, resentment, and fear. They can then begin to see themselves as individuals whose lives do not have to revolve around the moods and behavior of the drinker. They can explore their own needs, develop realistic attitudes, and begin to grow toward a new and lasting kind of health.

It is vital that family members make a painful examination of some of the losses to which they will have to adjust when (and if) the problem drinker stops abusing alcohol and changes his life. According to the systems theory, a change in any member of the family necessitates changes in the other members. When the drinker begins at last to build a new life, everyone else must make adjustments, and adjustments inevitably involve losses.

It is often difficult to convince family members that the long yearned for cessation of drinking will bring loss to them. Harold Swift and Terence Williams from the Hazelden Foundation offer three analogies that may help the family understand the very real kind of emotional loss the family suffers:

> Imagine, if you will, that you live in an apartment on a busy corner in the city, where sirens and traffic noises are a part of every day and night. Somehow, you learn to live with all but the loudest racket. Even if you don't rest well, you manage to sleep through each night. Then you go to the country for a holiday, hoping to find a few days of calmness, and you find that you can't sleep because it is too quiet. It's this kind of loss that we are talking about.
>
> Think of the ambiguous feelings some people have when children grow up and marry. They experience the relief of knowing that an important part of their life's work is done. They experience the joy of knowing that this person is entering a new life and assuming adult responsibilities. However, they may also feel a profound sadness about knowing the child is leaving home. And, there are the tears of separation.
>
> Another common example is the mixed blessing of retirement, especially from a job that finally has become difficult or unrewarding. Frequently, people look forward to retirement as a well-deserved reward for their years of labor, only to discover sadly that they have not prepared for all the losses that accompany the end of their daily work. They sometimes find themselves depressed, at loose ends.
>
> Losses like these have a bearing on the feelings that families experience, although the feelings may be hidden down inside, when addicts decide to grow up and take responsibility for themselves. The people in the noisy apartment — the parents letting go of a child whom they

really want to set free — workers retiring from sometimes tiresome jobs — all have something in common with the family of the addict: they are all facing loss of a burden. In this case, the burden of addiction has become a very important part of the way concerned persons look at themselves — of the way they define themselves. When the burden is no longer there, they are apt to feel that something is missing, while not believing their own feelings because they seem so illogical.[3]

The same authors describe more specifically five areas of family loss:

1. Loss of a Life-Style

During the drinking days, family members think of little except the drinker. They react continually to his destructive behavior, and he seems to absorb completely their entire lives. All thoughts and activities revolve around him.

If he decides to stop using alcohol, he becomes a "new" person, and the family loses its central member. The roles and relationships each person came to expect from everyone else change drastically, and the family members suffer from a painful loss of their familiar style of life.

2. Loss of Emotional Security

Although the relationship of the family to the drinker was a destructive one, it still involved a great deal of twisted emotional security. There was a certainty about the old relationship that made it attractive even with its accompanying pain. The drinker probably never admitted that he needed his family (indeed, he probably declared exactly the opposite), but they knew that he depended heavily upon them. This deep need, unhealthy though it was, gave them a sense of security.

During the drinking days, relationships became rigid and fixed to the point where no one needed ever to renegotiate them. The whole family knew the rules and was well aware of how everyone else would feel about a drinking episode and its aftermath.[4]

It is this false sense of emotional security that Drs. Mildred

Newman and Bernard Berkowitz speak of in their best seller, *How to Be Your Own Best Friend.*

> . . . there is also a hidden payoff in continuing to suffer.
> For one thing, it's familiar; we're very comfortable with it.
> It gives us a sense of security to keep on in the same old
> self-defeating ways, letting one bad action lead to another.
> We know what to expect. It makes our world
> comprehensible, predictable, in some sense manageable.[5]

When the drinker and his family finally enter treatment, they can begin to build a new, healthy foundation for emotional security. To accomplish this, however, they must relinquish their old, familiar relationships. This represents a very real and disturbing loss.

3. *Loss of Familiar Roles*

During the drinking days, the family learned various behaviors to help them deal with their seemingly insoluble problem. Even though their roles actually perpetuated the problem drinking, they became comfortable and familiar because each person could count on the others to behave in certain ways. Living conditions were miserable, but nonetheless, there was a security about them.

When the drinker stops using alcohol, the family must completely reorganize the innermost structure of the system. If the family works together, new, healthy roles will eventually evolve, but abandoning the old, familiar ways of behaving represents another important loss.

4. *Loss of the Scapegoat*

Creating a scapegoat is a form of displacement, a defense mechanism described earlier. Everyone has a tendency to disown unacceptable thoughts and feelings in himself and project them onto someone else (a scapegoat).

The family could easily blame everything that went wrong in their lives onto the drinker. Regardless of what troubled them, they were certain that the drinker was solely responsible. When he stops using alcohol, problems continue to arise, and the family learns, to its astonishment, that drinking did not cause all their pain. They must begin to deal directly and honestly with their problems and can no longer pin the blame on anyone else. Thus, they experience another bewildering loss.

5. Loss of False Esteem

When the drinker was using alcohol, family members received solace and comfort from friends, relatives, and neighbors. People remarked, "You're so brave and patient for putting up with that . . ." or "I don't know how you do it . . . you're a saint." This approval resulted in a false sense of self-esteem. If the drinker begins to recover, the attention shifts from the family to him and he begins to receive the praise. The family may unconsciously miss these ego-building statements and begin to resent the drinker for being the object of attention. [6]

Unless the family becomes aware of these losses and learns to deal effectively with them, members are sure to sabotage their own efforts to recover as a family. Treatment teaches them how to handle these changes.

Alcoholics Anonymous

Alcoholics Anonymous is a fellowship of recovering problem drinkers. It helps the drinker to change his negative ways of thinking and behaving and learn to live a whole new kind of life.

It is important that family and friends learn about A.A. and develop the right kind of attitudes about this vital organization.

Any worthwhile treatment program will certainly introduce the problem drinker to A.A. The fellowship has achieved greater success in helping problem drinkers than any other form of therapy.

The wife should enthusiastically encourage her husband to attend A.A. and join him for open meetings. Lewis Presnall, an occupational alcoholism consultant, lists five benefits a wife receives from going to A.A. with her husband:

- She will find herself in a fellowship of people who understand her problem.
- The second thing which the wife of the alcoholic will find in the fellowship is a continuing therapy for alcoholism.
- The third thing that the wife of the alcoholic will receive from the A.A. program is self-knowledge.
- The fourth thing that the wife of the alcoholic will gain from attendance at A.A. meetings is help with specific problems.
- In the A.A. group and the A.A. program the wife of the alcoholic can discover a satisfactory way of life.[7]

The wife's attendance at A.A. is just as important as that of her husband, especially if the couple lives in a community where there is no Al-Anon group.

If the problem drinker finds the help he needs in A.A., he may attend meetings four or five nights a week during the early stages of recovery. His wife should be extremely careful not to complain that he is gone every evening and to remember that for awhile, at least, he needs the additional support of several meetings a week.

Antabuse

Another kind of therapy which the spouse should understand thoroughly is the use of Antabuse to combat impulsive drinking. She may be suspicious of Antabuse because it is a drug, and drugs can be deadly for people who are learning to live contentedly without using chemicals to alter their moods. Many problem drinkers have lost their hard-won sobriety (and even their lives) by using pills. Antabuse is, however, an exception. Available only with a prescription, it has absolutely no effect upon the mood of a person. If the drinker takes Antabuse (the generic name is disulfiram), however, and then drinks alcohol, he will become extremely ill. A person may have a reaction to anything with an alcohol content (including cough syrup) for seven to ten days after he has taken Antabuse.

Reactions to the drug usually begin with a red, flushed skin. Heart palpitations, decreased blood pressure, and nausea follow quickly. The patient should go immediately to a hospital emergency room when a reaction starts. The severity of the response will depend upon the dose of Antabuse and the amount of alcohol the drinker has consumed. A very small amount of alcohol may produce little or no reaction.

The decision to take Antabuse is a serious one, and the drinker must make it freely after he determines to stop using alcohol. No one should give Antabuse to another person without his knowledge, by slipping it into his coffee or other surreptitious means.

Some patients may experience minimal side effects (which usually disappear after a few weeks) from the drug. These include skin reactions, drowsiness, and a metallic taste in the mouth. It may help to take the Antabuse at night rather than first thing in the morning.

As with any drug, there are certain substances which the patient should avoid while using Antabuse. Paraldehyde, Dilantin, Coumadin, and INH are some of them.

Antabuse is not for everyone. Diabetics, epileptics, psychotics, heart patients, and pregnant women should not receive the drug.

(If a person who is using Antabuse decides he simply must drink again, he should stop taking the drug and make up some alibi. "I ran out of it," or "It gives me ingrown toenails," are good excuses. He must then wait seven to ten days before he consumes any alcohol. If he decides to resume using Antabuse, he should allow about fifteen hours to elapse after his last drink before he takes his pill.)

Many people mistakenly believe that Antabuse causes sexual impotence. When a heavy drinker stops using alcohol, he may temporarily experience the devastating loss of his sexual powers. Drs. Smith, Lemere, and Dunn, in an article in *Northwest Medicine*, state that out of 17,000 patients treated for alcoholism, approximately 8 percent of the males suffered from impotence. (About 50 percent of this small number returned gradually to their previous level of sexual power.)[8] If a patient is taking Antabuse, he can conveniently blame his distress on the drug. Actually, his drinking is directly responsible for his impotence.

Antabuse is not a substitute for treatment. It is simply an adjunct to therapy. It cannot replace participation in A.A. or group or family counseling. If a person chooses to rely solely on Antabuse, he usually returns to drinking within a few months. Used properly, however, in conjunction with continuing therapy, Antabuse is an effective chemical shield which can be a tool for sobriety during the first few years of recovery.

Family members, especially the spouse, should remember that the problem drinker bears the total responsibility for taking Antabuse. No one else needs to get caught up in a destructive game of keeping track of whether or not he swallows his daily dose. If he stops using the drug, the family must realize that it is his decision and refuse to panic. A gentle reminder may help, but they should not continuously question him or try to insist that he take his pill. Families discover quickly that such an effort is utterly futile. The drinker will simply resort to subterfuge, perhaps by using substitutes which look like Antabuse or by holding the pill in his mouth and spitting it out later.

Dr. Don Damstra, a physician at St. Luke's Hospital in Phoenix, offers the following insight about what kind of problem drinkers respond well to Antabuse therapy:

> As far as the use of Antabuse is concerned, we can
> arbitrarily divide alcoholics into three groups. At one end
> of the scale are the alcoholics who are very highly
> motivated. They want very badly to be better. A person

with such tremendous motivation will probably not need Antabuse. He will have no significant use for it. If he does take Antabuse, it won't hurt him, however, because he is not going to drink anyway. It probably won't do him any good, but it will cause no harm.

At the other end of the continuum we have a group of alcoholics for whom Antabuse doesn't work because they won't take it. These drinkers don't have enough motivation to want to take the drug. They don't have enough of a desire to quit to bother with Antabuse.

Between these two extreme groups there are alcoholics who want very badly to get better, but seem to fail repeatedly. They are what a psychologist would call highly motivated. They sincerely desire to achieve sobriety, but they cannot. They try for awhile, and then begin drinking again.

These people need to get into a program like A.A. so they can grow and mature and lose their need to drink, but the process is gradual. Many of them fail to get into the program quickly enough to sustain their own sobriety. They go along without drinking for awhile and then they slip.

Such people may benefit from Antabuse because it provides a period of insured abstinence. They cannot drink while they are using the drug, and during this time, the process of personal growth has a chance to flourish. Antabuse will relieve the tension of deciding whether or not to drink.

We are all faced with having to live in a drinking society. People will continue to drink and we are going to come into contact repeatedly with alcoholic beverages all of our lives. Each time there is alcohol around us, we have to make a decision. Will we — or won't we — drink this time? With Antabuse, however, we make the decision only once a day. When we take the Antabuse, we need not even think about drinking, because we can't.

If we swallow it first thing in the morning before we have time to think about it, it relieves us of the pressure of making another decision that day.

Many people criticize Antabuse, declaring that we should not use it because it is a crutch. What real difference, however, does that make? A crutch is not necessarily bad. There are times when using a crutch is very appropriate.

The crutch of Antabuse can help support us while the healing process takes place.

Antabuse certainly takes all the fun out of drinking for the person who is an alcoholic and knows it. It destroys the enjoyment of the first few drinks or the first few days of a drinking bout. Antabuse completely demolishes any temporary pleasure left in alcohol.[9]

Summary

Whether the family chooses to reorganize with or without the drinker, it is imperative that they get some kind of help to heal their own wounds. Their need for treatment is as great as that of the drinker.

When all family members receive help, they have a unique opportunity to break through the defenses that each person is using and get back in touch with their innermost feelings. They gain valuable knowledge and begin to see clearly the formidable obstacles against which the family must fight. Only through this difficult process of healing does the family have a real chance to restore themselves to true and lasting health.

NOTES

Chapter VI

1. Don and Sharon Wegscheider, *Family Illness: Chemical Dependency*, p. 31.
2. Margaret R. Cork, *Alcoholism and the Family*, p. 7.
3. Harold A. Swift and Terence Williams, *Recovery for the Whole Family*, pp. 6–7.
4. *Ibid.*, pp. 7–8.
5. Mildred Newman and Bernard Berkowitz, *How to Be Your Own Best Friend* (paperback), p. 46. © 1971 by Mildred Newman and Bernard Berkowitz. Reprinted by permission of Random House, Inc.
6. Swift and Williams, *Recovery for the Whole Family*, p. 10.
7. Lewis F. Presnall, *Alcoholism — The Exposed Family*, pp. 1–5.
8. J. W. Smith, F. Lemere, and R. B. Dunn, "Impotence in Alcoholism," *Northwest Medicine*, pp. 523–524.
9. Don Damstra, "Antabuse" (Lecture delivered at Brighton Hospital, Brighton, Mich., 1968).

CHAPTER VII

The Family System Reorganizing

(Changing and Growing Together)

Treatment is the beginning of a long, difficult path of readjustment for the entire family. Sometimes it becomes painfully necessary for the family to pull itself together and reorganize without the problem drinker. He may insist upon continuing to abuse alcohol, forcing his wife to reach the unhappy conclusion that divorce is her only alternative. In other instances, the failure to get into treatment may be the tragic cause of his untimely death.

When both the drinker and his family enter a reliable, effective treatment program, however, there is every reason to hope that the drinking will cease and everyone involved will begin to learn a new, more satisfying way of life. This is no easy task, however, and there will be many lingering difficulties after treatment is complete.

This closing chapter will point out some of the major readjustments which the family must make if they are to restore balance and equilibrium to the system. They must work through residual feelings of mistrust, lowered self-esteem, left-over resentments, and a strong tendency to revert to "game playing" techniques. There will also be periods of severe stress and difficult situations which dangerously threaten the successful reorganization of the system.

Causes of Stress

The whole family has various expectations about the new roles which members are playing. Sometimes these expectations can cause a tremendous amount of anxiety and stress. The recovering problem drinker is eager to put into practice the tools for sobriety he has learned, but at the same time, he may be anxious about a possible relapse, the attitude of his employer, and the feelings of his old drinking friends. He is also concerned about how long it will take him to reassume the family responsibilities that once were his.

The rest of the family wonders:

"Is he going to drink again?"

"Is he angry with us for forcing him into treatment?"

"I don't know what to expect now that he is no longer drinking."

They may also ponder such questions as:

"Shall we keep liquor in the house at all?"

"Must we turn down invitations to social functions?"

"Will my husband be upset if I have a drink now and then?"

There is no pat answer to these difficult questions. Each family must talk them over and avoid extremes of overprotectiveness or of needless temptations.

In addition to these concerns and expectations, the problem drinker and other family members will suffer from periods of extreme stress during the reorganization and recovery process. It is important for the family to know about and understand the ramifications of these periods of stress. While the body rids itself of the physical presence of alcohol within twenty-four hours, "psychological detoxification" takes much longer. The anxiety and stress from which the drinker suffers reflect the extreme psychological dependency which remains long after alcohol is gone completely from the body.

After the trauma of physical withdrawal, the body has no need for alcohol, but the psychological craving lingers. During this time, anxiety and tension are psychological cues which cause an intense desire to drink. These stressful periods have various names. Valles refers to them as "BUD" periods, Scott calls them "flare-ups," and Solberg talks about the "dry drunk syndrome."

Symptoms of Stress Periods

Dr. Jorge Valles, a staff member at the VA Alcoholism Unit in Houston, Texas, described the "Building up to Drink (BUD)" period that will trouble the problem drinker and notes that other family members are usually able to recognize what is happening to the drinker before he himself becomes aware of it.[1] A BUD usually begins with the problem drinker feeling anxious, irritable, restless, depressed, resentful, or bored. Everyone experiences these emotions now and then, but in the recovering problem drinker, such symptoms can, if left unchecked, lead rapidly to a tragic resumption of drinking.

The BUD period may also manifest itself with a sudden change in mood, sleeplessness, a nervous stomach, a refusal to attend A.A. or take Antabuse, or by tension headaches or minor physical complaints. These symptoms grow more pronounced, and the person becomes either unreasonably quarrelsome or very quiet, withdrawing noticeably from the usual family conversations and interactions. Ultimately, a crisis situation causes the anxiety to become acute. The problem drinker may very well try to reduce his tension in the same way that was invariably successful in the past — he drinks alcohol. If he catches his distressing state of mind before he becomes "emotionally inebriated," however, he can deal effectively with it and avoid returning to alcohol.

If he learns to recognize his "BUD" period, the simple realization of what he is experiencing usually reduces his anxiety. (Treatment centers usually warn patients about these periods.) He knows the situation is temporary and that there are things he can do to help himself through it, such as contacting his sponsor or someone else who understands his condition. He should attend a few extra A.A. meetings, especially the "closed" ones, and discuss what is happening to him. Eating high protein foods such as hamburger, cheese, or ice cream, and taking part in physical activities (walking, swimming, or playing golf) may help.

Family members should be careful to retain their calmness during a BUD period. They should ask what they can do to alleviate stress for the problem drinker and continue to seek the help of Al-Anon and Alateen.

BUD periods can happen anytime, and may last from several days to several weeks. Bob Scott, Program Consultant at Raleigh Hills Hospital in California, uses the term "flare-ups" to describe these stressful times. He thinks they are fairly predictable and has found three especially dangerous periods during the first few years of recovery.

> The average alcoholic will experience his first stress period during the fifth to seventh week of sobriety. If he makes it through this, the feelings may recur again at five to seven months. Again, if he is successful in surviving this onslaught, it may recur at eleven to thirteen months. Some alcoholics experience all of these, and some have problems only during the eleventh to thirteenth month period. It must be remembered that the most natural, and therefore the most normal, response of the alcoholic to this stress is to return to drinking.[2]

Experts have recently added the eighteenth month as another dangerous time.

It is not only stress, tension, and anxiety that threaten the new-found sobriety of a recovering problem drinker. Periods of extreme elation or success, when everything is going marvelously, can be just as dangerous as the times of stress.

R. J. Solberg writes about a closely-related phenomenon, the "dry drunk syndrome." He describes the behavior of the problem drinker as grandiose and his attitude as rigidly judgmental. The drinker's moods swing erratically from agitation to depression. Like the other writers mentioned, Solberg stresses that it is extremely important for the drinker and the family to seek help immediately from outside sources such as counseling centers, Al-Anon Family Groups, and the A.A. sponsor.[3]

Charles Crewe, who was a therapist in the Aftercare Program at Hazelden, lists sixteen common symptoms, conditions, and attitudes that lead to "dry drunks" and possible relapses:

1. Exhaustion
2. Dishonesty
3. Impatience
4. Argumentativeness
5. Depression
6. Frustration
7. Self-Pity
8. Cockiness
9. Complacency
10. Expecting Too Much from Others
11. Letting up on Disciplines
12. Use of Mood-Altering Chemicals
13. Wanting Too Much
14. Forgetting Gratitude
15. "It Can't Happen to Me"
16. Omnipotence[4]

The drinker bears the primary responsibility of successfully working out his periods of stress. Although other family members inevitably suffer from the effects of these anxious times, all they can do is offer to help the drinker and continue in their own recovery program.

Aftercare

This discussion is not meant to discourage the family member who is coming home after treatment. Everyone concerned should, however, appreciate the magnitude of the problems and changes that are necessary if a healthy, well-functioning system is to emerge. It would, after all, be unrealistic to expect a short period of initial treatment to reverse completely all the destructive life-style patterns of the drinker as well as the inappropriate ways the family responded to these patterns. Changes of such magnitude require a great deal of time and work.

The road back to health and contentment has many potential chuckholes for the entire family. The chances of traveling this perilous journey successfully improve significantly if each member receives continuing care after initial treatment. This ongoing help is usually referred to as "aftercare," and it is just as important as the initial treatment period.

Aftercare provides a bridge from the initial treatment experience to the goal of a healthier family system. It offers the problem drinker and his loved ones the time and opportunity to find effective solutions to use when the old problems return. There are various types of aftercare (couples' groups, marital counseling groups, or growth groups), but regardless of the form it takes, it should be a supplement rather than a substitute for A.A. and Al-Anon.

Aftercare greatly increases the chances of a successful recovery for the family. There are, however, several other specific things a wife can do to help both herself and the reorganization of the family. She can:

1. *Continue to Attend Al-Anon Regularly*

   The fact that the drinker and the family have been through initial treatment is no reason to discontinue meetings. The wife needs Al-Anon now more than ever before. The fellowship can provide the extra support she needs to deal with the problems she will undoubtedly encounter in the reorganizational process. These problems include:

   a. Extreme Fatigue of the Drinker
      The drinker may experience continual exhaustion for weeks or months. What should the wife do with a husband who sleeps most of the time?
   b. Dry Drunks
   c. A Switch to Pills
      The drinker may consider taking tranquilizers, and she wonders, "Is it dangerous? What can I do about it?"

d. Feelings of Jealousy or Resentment
She may be angry that he spends every night at A.A.
meetings instead of home, or she may feel rejected because of a deteriorating sexual relationship.

Al-Anon can help with these problems. Slogans such as
"Easy Does It," "One Day at a Time," and "First Things First,"
suggest a relaxed attitude that can offer a needed solace from
the tensions of dealing with the ongoing difficulties of living
with a recovering problem drinker. Children should continue
to attend Alateen as well, for many the same reasons.

2. *Work on Communication*

Communication is the heartbeat of family relationships.
When the family became tangled in the web of problem
drinking, communication probably deteriorated to the
point where it almost ceased to exist. Treatment restored
the communication process somewhat, but during the
reorganizational phase, each family member has the opportunity to improve communication even more.

While communication is a complex subject, Al-Anon literature suggests five *guidelines* that family members can practice
in their communications with one another.

a. *"Discuss, Don't Attack"* When my husband was still drinking,
this rule saved lots of fights which could only make things
worse. But when he was sober, and real personality
problems came into focus, I certainly needed this rule.
The sober alcoholic is overly sensitive to criticism; and
when newly sober, his self-esteem is still fragile. He's so
braced for rejection that he imagines it even when it isn't
intended. Anything I might say that seems critical of him
as a person, would make him react emotionally and
defensively. If I have a grievance, I just tell him how I feel
about it. If it's a minor irritation and it still bothers me, I
sometimes say: "I know this is petty, but it gets to me
somehow, so I thought you'd want me to tell you about it."

b. *"Keep the Voice Low and Pleasant"* I had lots of experience
the other way, until I realized that when feelings run high,
voices get high — and then there's trouble. If something I
said got a loud-voiced reaction from him, I just left the

room. That made him more angry, of course, and for awhile he'd follow me and yell: "Don't you dare walk out on me when I'm talking to you!" But I finally convinced him, in a low voice, thank goodness, that our shouting days were over, and you'd be surprised at the difference in our home atmosphere!

c. *"Stick to the Subject"* When I started to tell him something, it seems I was always using the opportunity to list ten other things I'd been meaning to bring up. At last, I sat myself down and said: "One thing at a time is sufficient. If I confuse the issue, we'll end up fighting about his cousin Joe and my aunt Charlotte."

d. *"Listen to His Complaints"* When it's my turn to be on the receiving end of a complaint, I keep myself receptive to what he's saying, reminding myself that I want to be cool-headed, open-minded and reasonable. Maybe he's telling me something I need to know that will make me a better person. I don't answer his complaints about me with complaints about him.

e. *"Don't Make Demands"* I just state the case without telling him how I think it should be resolved. If he wants to do something about it, he's free to work out a solution of his own. If he doesn't, telling him what to do would be arguing about a solution instead of discussing the problem. By leaving the choice up to him, the door is open for a mutual coming to terms with the problem. Believe me, it was hard work to overcome my feeling that "my way is the only right way."[5]

3. *Continue Rational Self-Counseling*

By practicing this technique daily, she can assure herself of an emotionally more satisfying existence. Chapter IV discussed briefly the basic principles of this form of therapy. There are, however, a number of readable books available to those who wish to pursue the subject further.

A wife must remember that it takes daily practice for several weeks or months to break self-defeating thinking patterns and to relearn attitudes that are rational, sensible, and realistic. She has nothing to lose but her bad feelings. It was probably a spouse who was diligently practicing all these suggestions who wrote:

When my husband came home, we learned to be honest with each other. We don't do things behind each other's backs. We are working as a team instead of as two individuals scheming against each other. Since my husband has been sober in A.A., I realize again what a truly fine person he is. I had completely blocked this out of my mind when he was drinking. Now, if my husband lapses into drinking again, I will remember I am powerless over alcohol and that there is nothing I can do to change him. I can only help him to want to change by changing myself. The children and I won't have to hide in closets or pack and leave the house for the night. We'll just go on as if nothing out of the ordinary had happened.

There are still days when I feel myself slipping back into my old ways, and usually I can pull myself out of them by calling a few of my Al-Anon friends on the telephone. At other times, I just have a lapse that lasts until I become aware that I wasn't practicing the Al-Anon program enough. I need Al-Anon meetings whether my husband is drinking or not. This is my road back to serenity and a normal life. Whatever happens, it is today that counts. We are going to make the most of it and enjoy it and, with the help of God, live it as best we can.[6]

The Wegscheiders express effectively what happens to a family system when all of its members work honestly and patiently at repatterning their relationships:

When a family has finished its treatment program and is actively pursuing its rehabilitation program, we see a different picture. We see a family as a group who are fully themselves, not perfect, but aware of who they are at that time. They are conscious of their inadequacies and fears as well as their talents and gifts. Each is allowed to be himself, even if that means that he is different. Each feels free to express feelings openly. Each realizes that change is a part of life, and sometimes a sign of life. A functional family has its share of pains and joys. When a member says he is happy or sad, he looks it, he is believable. They are a group of people who know that they belong, and continually choose to belong, to each other. Each of their identities is his own. Their relationships depend on who they are rather than on performance. They are centered on wholeness and in touch with reality.[7]

NOTES

Chapter VII

1. Jorge Valles, *How to Live with an Alcoholic* (paperback), pp. 107–115.
2. B. Scott, E. W. Fitz, and K. H. Walker, "Flare-ups: Stress Times in Recovery from Alcoholism," *Osteopathic Physician*, pp. 49–60.
3. R. J. Solberg, *Dry Drunk Syndrome*, p. 7.
4. Charles W. Crewe, *A Look at Relapse*, pp. 6–8.
5. *The Dilemma of the Alcoholic Marriage*, pp. 31–33.
6. *Homeward Bound*, pp. 7–8.
7. Don and Sharon Wegscheider, *Family Illness: Chemical Dependency*, p. 40.

Epilogue

If a spouse has done everything this book suggests and her husband still refuses to seek treatment, she has a choice to make. There are two alternatives open to her, illustrated by the following case histories:

Mary Jo and Nancy were in similar situations. Both had been married for ten to twelve years, both had two small children, and both had a husband with a drinking problem. In spite of continuing efforts of the wives to intervene, both men refused to seek treatment.

Mary Jo and Nancy were fearful and reluctant to dissolve their marriages. Such drastic action meant giving up their false security and facing the uncertainty of making it on their own.

Mary Jo decided to remain with her husband. To this day, he continues to drink. She complains and threatens to leave, but she never will. She lives continually with the delusion that someday he will change. Meanwhile, she is a nervous wreck and admits readily that she is very unhappy. She refuses, however, to withdraw from the sick family system. She will not admit it, but despite counseling, her children also manifest neurotic behavior as a result of living in constant fear and insecurity.

Nancy, on the other hand, decided to risk the uncertainty of making it on her own when her husband refused treatment. She refused to be victimized any longer, and ended her marriage.

Things were rough for her and the children for awhile, but they weathered the storm of readjustment. The children appear to be emotionally healthy, and they are beginning to build new lives for themselves. Nancy thinks it is unfortunate that she could not salvage her marriage, but she concludes, "I did the best I could, and now it's his problem."

Like the problem drinker, the wife must take responsibility for her own recovery. She and her children deserve a chance to live in a normal, healthy environment, which they will never find if they continue to exist in a family where there is alcohol abuse. It is a clear choice: a victim — or a victim no more.

Bibliography

Alateen: Hope for the Children of Alcoholics. New York: Al-Anon Family Group Headquarters, 1973.

Alcoholism and the Family. Fairfield Plan, no. 5. Cos Cob: National Council on Alcoholism, Southwestern Connecticut Area, 1975.

Bates, Richard C. *How Alcoholic Patients Can Help Themselves.* Cassette Tape. Chicago: Teach 'Em, 1975.

Berne, Eric. *Games People Play.* New York: Grove Press, 1964.

Booz, Allen, and Hamilton, Inc. *Final Report on the Needs of and Resources for Children of Alcoholic Parents.* Prepared for the National Institute on Alcohol Abuse and Alcoholism. Rockville, MD, National Institute on Alcohol Abuse and Alcoholism, 1974.

Bowen, Murray. "A Family Systems Approach to Alcoholism." Addictions 21, no. 2 (1974): 28–39.

Casey B. and McMullin, R. *Talk Sense to Yourself.* Wheatridge, CO: Jefferson County Mental Health Center, 1975.

Chafetz, Morris E.; Blane, Howard T.; and Hill, Marjorie J. "Children of Alcoholics: Observations in a Child Guidance Clinic." *Quarterly Journal of Studies on Alcohol* 32 (1971): 687–698.

Cork, R. Margaret. *Alcoholism and the Family.* Toronto: Addiction Research Foundation, 1971.

———. *The Forgotten Children.* Toronto: Paper Jacks, Addiction Research Foundation, 1969.

Coudert, Jo. *The Alcoholic in Your Life.* New York: Stein and Day, 1972.

Couture, Josie. "News Bulletin." New York: Other Victims of Alcoholism, 1977.

Crewe, Charles W. *A Look at Relapse*. Center City, MN: Hazelden, 1973.

Damstra, Don. "Antabuse." Lecture delivered at Brighton Hospital, Brighton, MI, 1968.

Dilemma of the Alcoholic Marriage. New York: Al-Anon Family Group Headquarters, 1971.

Edwards, Patricia; Harvey, Cheryl; and Whitehead, Paul D. "Wives of Alcoholics: A Critical Review and Analysis." *Quarterly Journal of Studies on Alcohol* 34 (1973): 112–132.

Ellis, Albert and Harper, Robert A. *A New Guide to Rational Living*. Hollywood: Wilshire Book Company, 1976.

Fajardo, Roque. *Helping Your Alcoholic before He or She Hits Bottom*. New York: Crown Publishers, 1976.

Fox, Ruth. "The Alcoholic Spouse." *Neurotic Interaction in Marriage*, edited by V. Eisenstein. New York: Basic Books, 1956.

Goldberg, Martin. "Chronic Alcoholism: Include the Alcoholic and the Spouse in Treatment." *Consultant*, November, 1974, pp. 63–69.

Gooderham, Melville. "The Therapy of Relationships." *Addictions* 19, no. 4 (1972): 58–62.

Goodman, David S. *Emotional Well-Being through Rational Behavior Training*. Springfield, IL: Charles C. Thomas, 1974.

Grimmett, John O. *Barriers against Recovery*. Center City, MN: Hazelden, 1973.

Grossack, Martin. *You Are Not Alone*. Boston: Marlborough House, 1965.

Hauck, Paul. *Overcoming Depression*. Philadelphia: Westminster Press, 1973.

———. *Overcoming Frustration and Anger*. Philadelphia: Westminster Press, 1974.

———. *Overcoming Worry and Fear*. Philadelphia: Westminster Press, 1975.

Heilman, Richard O. *Dynamics of Drug Dependency*. Center City, MN: Hazelden, 1973.

Hindman, Margaret. "Child Abuse and Neglect: The Alcohol Connection." *Alcohol Health and Research World* 1, no. 3 (1977): 2–7.

———. "Family Therapy in Alcoholism." *Alcohol Health and Research World* 1, no. 1 (1976): 2–9.

Homeward Bound. New York: Al-Anon Family Group Headquarters, 1968.

Hubbell, J. "A Dynamic New Approach to the Alcoholic." *Readers Digest*, May, 1976, pp. 173–177.

I'll Quit Tomorrow. Training manual for film. Minneapolis: Johnson Institute, 1977.

Intervention. Minneapolis: Johnson Institute, n.d.

Jackson, Joan K. "The Adjustments of the Family to the Crisis of Alcoholism." *Quarterly Journal of Studies on Alcohol* 15 (1954): 562–586.

102   Victims No More

James, Jane E. and Goldman, Morton. "Behavior Trends of Wives of Alcoholics." *Quarterly Journal of Studies on Alcohol* 32 (1971): 373–381.

Johnson, Vernon E. *I'll Quit Tomorrow.* New York: Harper and Row, 1973.

Keller, John. *Alcohol. A Family Affair.* Santa Ynez, CA: Kroc Foundation, 1977.

Kellermann, Joseph L. *Alcoholism: A Merry-go-round Named Denial.* Center City, MN: Hazelden, 1973.

Kimball, Bonnie-Jean. *Aftercare: Blueprint for a Richer Life.* Center City, MN: Hazelden, 1976.

Krimmel, Herman and Spears, Helen. *The Effect of Parental Alcoholism on Adolescents.* Cleveland: Center on Alcoholism, 1964.

Kübler-Ross, Elisabeth. *On Death and Dying.* New York: Macmillan, 1969.

Lembo, John. *Help Yourself.* Chicago: Argus Communications, 1974.

Mann, Marty. *Marty Mann Answers Your Questions about Drinking and Alcoholism.* New York: Holt, Rinehart and Winston, 1970.

———. *Marty Mann's New Primer on Alcoholism.* New York: Holt, Rinehart and Winston, 1958.

Maultsby, Maxie. *Help Yourself to Happiness through Rational Self Counseling.* Boston: Herman Publishers, 1975.

Maxwell, Ruth. *The Booze Battle.* New York: Praeger, 1976.

Meeks, Donald E. and Kelly, Coleen. "Family Therapy of Recovering Alcoholics." *Quarterly Journal of Studies on Alcohol* 31 (1970): 399–413.

Newman, Mildred and Berkowitz, Bernard. *How to Be Your Own Best Friend.* New York: Ballantine, 1974.

Orford, Jim *et. al.* "Self-Reported Coping Behavior of Wives of Alcoholics and Its Association with Drinking Outcome." *Journal of Studies on Alcohol* 36 (1975): 1254–1267.

Presnall, Lewis F. *Alcoholism — The Exposed Family.* Salt Lake City: Utah Alcoholism Foundation, n.d.

Recovery of Chemically Dependent Families. Minneapolis: Johnson Institute, n.d.

Reddy, Betty. *Alcoholism: A Family Illness.* Park Ridge, IL: Lutheran General Hospital, 1973.

Reilly, Richard. *America's Worst Drug Problem: Alcohol.* Liguori, MO: Liguori Publications, 1974.

Scott, B.; Fitz, E. W.; and Walker, K. H. "Flare-ups: Stress Times in Recovery from Alcoholism." *Osteopathic Physician*, February, 1969, pp. 49–60.

Smith, J. W.; Lemere, F.; and Dunn, R. B. "Impotence in Alcoholism." *Northwest Medicine* 71 (1972): 523–524.

Solberg, R. J. *Dry Drunk Syndrome.* Center City, MN: Hazelden, 1973

Steiner, Claude. *Games Alcoholics Play.* New York: Grove Press, 1971.

———. "Games of Alcoholics and Their Therapists." *Proceedings of the Second Annual Alcoholism Conference of the National Institute on Alcohol Abuse and Alcoholism*, Rockville, MD: National Institute on Alcohol Abuse and Alcoholism, 1972.

Swift, Harold A. and Williams, Terence. *Recovery for the Whole Family*. Center City, MN: Hazelden, 1975.

This Is Al-Anon. New York: Al-Anon Family Group Headquarters, 1967.

Tiebout, Harry M. *Surrender Versus Compliance in Therapy with Special Reference to Alcoholism*. Greenwich, CT: National Council on Alcoholism, 1952.

Valles, Jorge. *How to Live with an Alcoholic*. New York: Essandess Specials, Simon and Schuster, n.d.

Ward, Robert and Faillace, Louis. "The Alcoholic and His Helpers: A Systems View." *Quarterly Journal of Studies on Alcohol* 31 (1970): 684–691.

Wegscheider, Don and Sharon. *Family Illness: Chemical Dependency*. Minneapolis: Johnson Institute, 1975.

Weinberg, Jon R. *Why Do Alcoholics Deny Their Problem?* Center City, MN: Hazelden, 1973.

Whalen, Thelma. "Wives of Alcoholics: Four Types Observed in a Family Service Agency." *Quarterly Journal of Studies on Alcohol* 14 (1953): 632–641.

What Do You Do about the Alcoholic's Drinking? New York: Al-Anon Family Group Headquarters, 1966.

Why Haven't I Been Able to Help? Minneapolis: Johnson Institute, n.d.

Williams, Terence. *Free to Care*. Center City, MN: Hazelden, 1975.

Young, Howard S. *A Rational Counseling Primer*. New York: Institute for Rational Living, 1974.

Zink, Muriel. *So Your Alcoholic Is Sober*. Minneapolis: CompCare Publications, 1976.

Zink, Muriel. *Ways to Live More Comfortably with Your Alcoholic*. Minneapolis: CompCare Publications, 1976.